TORIE JAYNE'S
Stylish Home Sewing

D1486589

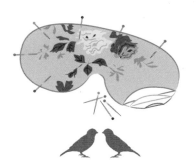

Torie Jayne's
Stylish Home Sewing

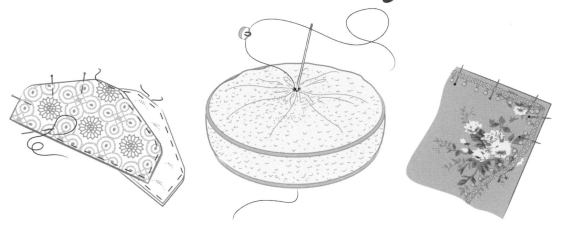

OVER 35 SEWING PROJECTS TO
MAKE YOUR HOME BEAUTIFUL

CICO BOOKS
LONDON NEW YORK

I dedicate my first sewing book to my home economics teacher, aka my mum.

Published in 2015 by CICO Books
An imprint of Ryland Peters & Small Ltd
20-21 Jockey's Fields   341 E 116th St
London WC1R 4BW   New York, NY 10029

www.rylandpeters.com

10 9 8 7 6 5 4 3 2 1

Text © Torie Jayne 2015
Design and photography ©
CICO Books 2015

The author's moral rights have been asserted. All rights reserved. No part of this publication may be reproduced, stored in a retrieval system, or transmitted in any form or by any means, electronic, mechanical, photocopying, or otherwise, without the prior permission of the publisher.

A CIP catalog record for this book is available from the Library of Congress and the British Library.

ISBN: 978 1 78249 193 4

Printed in China

Editor Alison Wormleighton
Designer Sarah Rock
Photographer Sussie Bell
Illustrator Kate Simunek
Stylist Torie Jayne

Managing editor Gillian Haslam
In-house designer Fahema Khanam
Art director Sally Powell
Production controller Mai-Ling Collyer
Publishing manager Penny Craig
Publisher Cindy Richards

For digital editions, visit www.cicobooks.com/apps.php

All projects provide both metric and standard/imperial measurements. Please use only one set when cutting out and sewing as they are not interchangeable.

ACKNOWLEDGMENTS I love this bit, the place I get to thank all the people who made this dream a reality.

So a big, warm, heartfelt thanks goes to Cindy Richards of Cico Books for suggesting I write a sewing book, and Gillian Haslam, my editor, who has been a constant pillar of support and understanding and kept me going even when my computer broke! To Alison Wormleighton for making sense of my instructions and Kate Simunek for her beautiful illustrations. A huge big thanks to Sussie Bell, in my opinion the best photographer in the world, for bringing my creations to life in her gorgeous photographs and who kindly opened up her home so we could shoot a lot of the projects there while we continued to renovate our new home in the country.

To the amazingly helpful Sooz of Sooz Custom Clothing in Okehampton, whose advice and help were and continue to be priceless. A big thanks to Bombay Duck for providing the cake stand, jewelry holder, and polka dot plates. To Plastikote for providing the spray paint to makeover my chairs, Ronseal for providing paint to makeover my summerhouse, and Laura Ashley for providing the oilcloth fabric and the garden paint for my deckchairs.

To my mum and dad for their constant encouragement and for all their tireless help in getting my garden ready for the garden shoot. To my friends Emma and Lucy for helping out on the photo shoots. To my Torie Jayne readers and blogging friends, who light up my life and keep me going on my new creative journey.

Always last on my list but always first on my mind, my amazing Keiran, whose unwavering daily support, love, laughter, and encouragement made this possible.

contents

Introduction

I used to love sewing as a child and was delighted when my grandmother gave me an old Singer sewing machine that was operated by turning the wheel. I used to spend hours making clothes for my dolls and gifts for my family. After my degree in fashion design, where I did a lot of sewing on industrial machines, I was thankful when I got my first job that I wouldn't actually have to do any of the sewing myself for a while!

My love affair with sewing has been re-ignited over the past few years, as I've made curtains and shades for my windows, patchwork pillows, felt bird decorations, bunting, and my favorite, a children's wigwam for my nephews. I am therefore absolutely delighted to be sharing with you my first sewing book, full of simple projects that have clear, step-by-step instructions and beautiful photography, making it easy to create your own desirable home furnishings and accessories.

The book is organized into chapters corresponding to the rooms found in a typical home—entrance, kitchen and dining room, living room, laundry room, and bedroom—and it also includes ideas for outdoor spaces. Each chapter has projects that I designed and made for my own home. However, most of the sewing projects would work well in lots of different situations. For example, the ottoman pouf has an oilcloth base, making it equally at home in the living room or on the patio. Many of the projects include variations so that, with a few tweaks, you can turn a project for, say, a small make-up bag into one for a stylish tote.

I have designed each and every project around my own home's color palette and style, showing you how easy it is to achieve a pretty, coordinated look that you can easily replicate or change to suit your own style and taste.

Chapter 1

Getting started

The specific techniques used in this book are explained in detail in each project, but here is the background information you need to know to do the projects.

Sewing kit

You don't need an enormous sewing kit to make the projects in this book: just a sewing machine, an iron, dressmaker's shears, small pointy scissors, a seam ripper, a measuring tape, a long straightedge, and pins and needles. You'll also need embroidery floss (thread) for many of my projects; I prefer the stranded cotton type, which I normally use without separating the six strands.

A sewing machine needle that does not properly penetrate the fabric while the stitches are being created can cause stitching to look crooked or like a narrow zigzag stitch. Using the correct needle for the fabric you are sewing is an important part of enabling the sewing machine to form beautiful stitching. The size of a needle is calculated by its diameter, so, for example, a 100 needle is 1mm in diameter. For the heavyweight cotton projects in this book, I recommend you use a 100 needle, and for the lightweight cotton, voile, and eyelet (broderie anglaise) fabric a 70 needle.

I also recommend the following additions to your sewing kit, which are not essential but are really useful:

A ROTARY CUTTER, used with a metal straightedge and a cutting mat, is handy when cutting out patchwork pieces.

PINKING SHEARS can be used to cut out fabric with an edge that is less prone to fraying and also looks pretty.

A WATER-SOLUBLE MARKER is much easier to use on fabric than a pencil and is also easier to see. The great thing is that markings can be removed with clean water or by gentle rubbing with a clean, damp cloth when you are finished.

A DRESSMAKER'S PENCIL is good for marking accurately. It often comes in a pack of three, including a white one, a dark one, and a bright one, to show up on any fabric. Some types can be removed with water, some fade away over time, and some can be brushed off.

A QUILTING FOOT for your machine ensures that thick fabrics or multiple layers feed through evenly, ensuring even stitching. It may include a detachable quilting bar to use as a stitching guide.

A TEFLON (NON-STICK) FOOT for your machine helps prevent fabrics such as leather, oilcloth, vinyl, plastic, and suede from sticking to the bottom of the foot and to the foot plate of the machine.

FRAY-STOP LIQUID prevents raw edges from fraying. I like to use it on the ends of ribbons so that they don't need hemming.

BASTING SPRAY is an adhesive spray that allows you to baste quilt layers together instantly. I use 505 basting spray, as it does not gum up needles or scissors. The adhesive bond that holds the quilt layers together is temporary, allowing you to reposition the layers as necessary. It will release when washed; otherwise, it will last about two months for polyester and about four months for natural fibers and blends.

A CHOPSTICK is ideal for pushing out stitched corners, as it is stiff enough for tough corners but not so sharp that it will make a hole in the fabric.

Basic techniques

Transferring templates

All the templates used in this book can be found on pages 136-143. Simply photocopy the templates, enlarging them if necessary (indicated on the template). Sections of larger templates may need to be taped together (also indicated). Pin the photocopied template to your fabric (drawing around it if you wish), and then cut around it (or along the drawn line). The templates indicate whether a seam allowance is included. If the template has markings, transfer them using a water-soluble marker, dressmaker's pencil, or pins. For templates you will use over and over again, such as the petals of the Felt Flower Pillow (page 68), you may prefer to stick the photocopied template to cardstock or cardboard.

Cutting out fabric

Cut on a hard surface such as a large table, using dressmaker's shears. It's advisable to wash all your fabrics before starting on the projects, to preshrink them. Always press fabric before cutting it out, which helps you cut accurately.

Fabric can be folded in various ways before pattern pieces are positioned for cutting. It is often folded in half lengthwise with selvages matching, but lengthwise folds can also be partial folds, leaving some of the fabric extended as a single layer, to use the fabric economically; in that case, you need to make sure that the fold is exactly on the grain, so measure the distance between the selvages at the ends to make sure they are the same.

Check whether any templates are to be placed on the fabric fold. When cutting out these pieces, never cut along the folded edge. Instead, fold the fabric and place the fold line exactly against that of the fabric.

Lay all templates on the fabric before pinning them in place, to make sure they will fit. Place the templates so any grain-line arrows run lengthwise. To check this, measure from the arrow to the fabric selvage—the measurement should be the same at both ends. If the fabric has a direction (either in the nap, as in corduroy or velvet, or in the print), check that the pieces run in the same direction. Now pin the templates to the fabric, placing the pins inside the cutting line; at corners, place pins diagonally.

Machine stitching

Here are the types of machine stitching referred to in this book.

STRAIGHT STITCH is your basic utility stitch that is used throughout. On most sewing machines the straight stitch length can be adjusted from zero to 5.0, which means that the largest stitches are each 1/4in (5mm) long. Adjusting the stitch length can eliminate puckered seams and improve the overall appearance. When sewing seams, use a straight stitch setting of 2.0-2.5, depending on the fabric.

BACKSTITCHING by machine involves sewing a few stitches in reverse at the beginning or end of a seam to anchor the seam and prevent stitches coming undone.

EDGE STITCHING is a straight stitch sewn from the right side of the fabric, 1/16-1/8in (1.5-3mm) from the edge, or from a seam line, or from another stitching line, to anchor, reinforce, or finish it. When edge stitching, you may be able to use the edge of your presser foot as a stitching guide.

TOPSTITCHING is a straight stitch sewn from the right side of the fabric, either for visual purposes or to hold something in place. It tends to be at least 3/8in (1cm) from an edge, seam, or another stitching line, and parallel to it. The thread can be either matching or contrasting.

BASTING (TACKING) is a long stitch used to temporarily hold together layers of fabric during construction. Machine basting is done by setting the machine to its longest straight stitch. (For hand basting, see page 10.)

STAYSTITCHING is a single line of medium-length straight machine stitches just inside the seam line, done before you join a piece of fabric to another piece. It is principally used to prevent curved or bias edges from stretching when seamed. However, it is also helpful when you have to clip into a seam allowance prior to seaming, because it helps prevent you from snipping beyond the seam line. There is no need to remove it after a seam is stitched because it isn't visible and it will act as a permanent aid to prevent stretching.

Stitching seams

The distance from stitching to edge of the fabric is called the seam allowance. Seam allowances in this book are usually ³⁄₈in (1cm), or ¾in (2cm) if a zipper is to be applied to the seam. For fine work where strength is not important, a ¼in (5mm) seam allowance is sometimes used.

For a professional finish, seams must be sewn straight, which means you need a seam guide on your machine. The seam guide aligns with the edge of the fabric so the stitching will create the correct seam allowance and keep it even. Most machines have adjustable seam guides—otherwise, you can stick tape in the correct position.

Conventional seams are stitched on two pieces of fabric placed right sides together, so seam allowances are hidden when the fabric is turned right side out. However, bound seams (see page 12), which I use a lot, are often stitched wrong sides together, because the binding will cover the seam allowances. If your fabric has no obvious right or wrong side, you can designate either as the right side.

PIVOTING FABRIC AT CORNERS involves changing the stitching direction at a corner or another angled point in the stitching line. For example, if you need to turn a corner in a ³⁄₈in (1cm) seam, the pivot point is ³⁄₈in (1cm) from the edge of the fabric at the corner. To pivot, stop with the needle down in the fabric when you arrive at the pivot point, and lift the presser foot. Then pivot (rotate) the fabric to the new stitching position, lower the presser foot, and continue stitching.

PRESSING SEAMS is done after sewing them. First press the seam flat to embed the stitches. Then, depending on the project instructions, you can either press the seam allowances open (in opposite directions away from the seam line) or together to one side.

Finishing seam allowances

A seam finish prevents fabric fraying and can add strength to a seam. In this book I have finished raw edges by binding (see Binding an Edge, page 12), pinking (trimming with pinking shears—see page 8), or, most often, zigzagging.

ZIGZAGGING is a machine stitch that changes direction with each stitch, creating a zigzag effect, and is ideal for finishing raw edges. Fit the machine with the zigzag foot if it is different from the regular foot. Set the machine to a short length and a medium stitch width, and stitch slightly in from the raw edge. Trim away the excess fabric outside the zigzagging, being careful not to clip into the stitching. Seam allowances are normally zigzagged separately, but if the project instructions tell you to press the seam allowances to one side, they can be zigzagged either separately or together.

CLIPPING CURVES is done on shaped seams to make them lie flat. On an outward (convex) curve, make straight snips into the seam allowance at right angles to the seam line using sharp, pointy scissors. On an inward (concave) curve, cut little wedge shapes. Take care not to cut through the stitching.

SNIPPING OFF CORNERS of seam allowances reduces bulk and allows for crisp corners. Cut off the triangular pieces close to the seam line, being careful not to cut through the stitches.

Running stitch and hand basting

Running stitch is a straight hand stitch that can be used for gathering small amounts of fabric and also for decoration. Sew small, evenly spaced stitches in a straight line by bringing the needle up through the fabric and taking it down several times, then pulling the thread through, before repeating the process. Hand basting, which is used to hold layers of fabric together while stitching, consists of long running stitches, about ¼-³⁄₈in (5mm-1cm) in length.

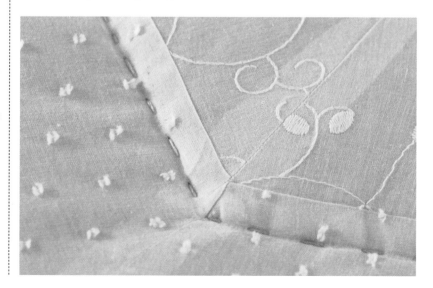

Slipstitching an opening

Slipstitch is often used to create an invisible seam between two folded edges, particularly when sewing openings closed.

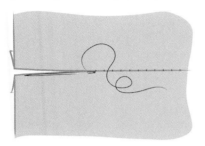

1 Thread a hand needle and knot the two thread ends together. Turn in the seam allowances of the opening and press the folds flat. Slip the needle inside one of the folds, to hide the knot. Bring the needle out through the fold and pull the thread through. Insert the needle into the other fold, directly opposite or no more than 1-2mm farther along. Slide it along by about ⅛-¼in (3–5mm), and then bring it back out. Insert it into the fold opposite, again no more than 1-2mm farther along. Continue to the end of the opening.

2 At the end, gently pull the thread to tighten the stitches, so that they are concealed between the two sides of the seam. To finish, use the needle to pick up a tiny section of the seam opposite where the thread emerges, pass the needle and thread through this loop, and pull tight to form a knot. Snip off the ends of the thread.

Slipstitching a hem

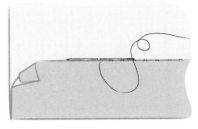

Also known as slip hemming, this method uses slipstitch to invisibly sew a folded edge to a flat piece, such as sewing a hem in place. Follow the instructions for Slipstitching an Opening (see left) but instead of sliding the needle inside a second fold, pick up only three threads in the flat piece.

Making bias tape

Readymade bias tape (bias binding) can be purchased in various widths, colors, and prints, but making your own gives you more choice. Because the tape is cut on the bias (at a 45-degree angle to the fabric's grain line) it allows you to bind curved edges and to wrap it around piping cord, but it can also be used on straight edges.

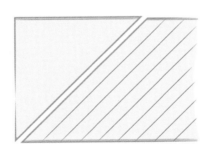

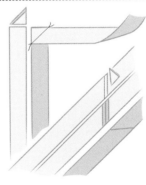

1 First decide on the cut width of the tape. If you are using it for binding, you'll need twice the finished width (the width of the tape visible from the front after binding the edge), plus two seam allowances. In this book, many of the projects use bias tape with a finished width of ½in (15mm), and most of the seam allowances are ⅜in (1cm), so the cut width should be 1¾in (5cm). If you are using the bias tape for piping, wrap some fabric around the cord—you'll need this width plus two seam allowances.

2 Fold your fabric on the diagonal, so that one selvage is exactly at right angles to the other. Press along the diagonal fold, then unfold the fabric and draw lines on the wrong side, parallel to the diagonal crease line. The distance between the lines should be the desired cut width of your bias tape. Draw enough lines to give you the total length you need, then cut along the lines.

3 To make it easier to join the strips, square up the ends (i.e., trim off the triangle at each end). Place the ends of two strips at a 90-degree angle, right sides together. Stitch along the diagonal of the square formed by where they overlap. Repeat for the remaining strips, making sure seams all slant in the same direction. Trim seam allowances to ¼in (5mm) and press seams open. If using bias tape for binding, fold the long edges in toward the center by the amount of the seam allowance, and press along both fold lines; there is no need to make these folds for piping.

Binding an edge

This is a useful and decorative way to finish an edge, whether you are using it instead of a seam to join layers, or simply binding the edge of a single layer. You can either buy readymade bias tape (bias binding) or make your own (see page 11). Many of my projects use ½in- (15mm-) wide bias tape for binding an edge, which refers to the amount visible from the front when the process is completed; the tape is wider than that when it is opened out. Readymade tape is either "single-fold," which means it has both raw edges folded in, or "double-fold", which has an additional fold down the center (it is actually slightly off-center).

1 Open out one side of the bias tape (the narrower side if there is an off-center fold) and turn in ¼in (5mm) at the

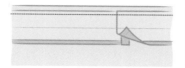

starting end. Pin the right side of the tape to the front of the fabric, the tape seam line (the fold near the edge) aligning with the fabric seam line. If there are finished edges at the ends of the edge you are binding, turn under the finishing end of the tape; but if the finishing end meets the starting point, as illustrated here, lap it over the turned-in starting end without turning in the finishing end. Stitch along the seam line.

2 Flip the bias tape up and press it away from the seam line. Now take it over the raw edge to the back of the fabric and pin

the other folded edge of the tape to the back so that it just covers the stitching. You may need to trim the fabric seam allowance if it is wider than the folded tape or very bulky.

3 Topstitch the tape in place from the front, making sure the stitching goes through the folded edge of the tape on the back. If you prefer no stitching to be visible from

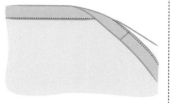

the front, you could either "stitch in the ditch" (machine stitch in the groove on the front just alongside the binding) or slipstitch the tape to the back, as for Slipstitching a Hem, page 11.

Piping an edge

Piping consists of a folded strip of bias fabric, usually with piping cord inside it. When thick cord is used, the piping is often called welting. The bias strips can be readymade or homemade bias tape (see Making Bias Tape, page 11).

1 Wrap the bias tape, right side out, around the cord. With the raw edges even, pin and then machine baste close to the cord, with the zipper foot or piping foot on your machine.

2 Starting at an inconspicuous place, pin the piping around the edge of one piece of fabric on the right side, with the piping facing inward, and the basting just inside the seam line.

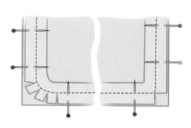

The raw edges will be even if the seam allowances of the piping and the project are the same. At corners and on curves, clip into the seam allowance of the piping.

3 Using the zipper foot or piping foot, machine baste along the previous basting line. If the end meets the beginning of the piping, leave 2in (5cm) unstitched at each end, remove the basting at

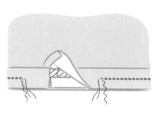

one end, and pull back the bias tape. Trim the cord so that the ends butt up, then turn under one end of the bias tape and lap it over the other end as you wrap the bias tape around the cord; machine baste.

4 Pin the piped piece of fabric to the other piece, with right sides together and raw edges even. With the zipper foot or piping foot still on the machine, stitch along the seam line, hugging the cord, through all four layers.

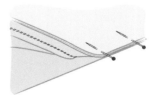

Applying a zipper

This is the simplest and most versatile way to apply a zipper. It is easiest to apply early in the project, when the fabric can be opened out flat.

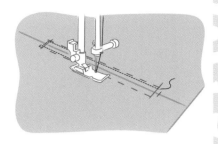

1 Finish the raw edges of the fabric by zigzagging them separately. Pin one edge to the other, right sides together and raw edges even. Lay the zipper along the pinned edges in the position required—such as centered between the top and bottom of the seam, or at one end. Mark on the seam allowances the top and bottom of the zipper—just above the zipper pull at the top and just below the zipper stay at the bottom.

2 Set the zipper aside and stitch a seam of the specified width as far as the first mark; in this book, the seam allowance for seams with zippers is ¾in (2cm). Backstitch two or three stitches, then machine baste along the seam line as far as the other mark. Begin stitching with a normal stitch length again at this mark, and after a few stitches, backstitch two or three stitches, then continue stitching to the end. Press the seam open.

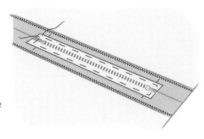

3 Place the closed zipper face down over the seam allowances, matching the top and bottom of the zipper to your markings and ensuring that the teeth line up with the seam line; pin. Hand baste all around the zipper through all layers. Remove the pins. Turn the fabric over and use pins or a water-soluble marker to mark the top and bottom of the zipper (as in step 1) on the right side.

4 With a zipper foot and working from the right side of the fabric, start at the top mark and stitch ¼in (5mm) from the opening edge. When you reach the bottom marking, stop with the needle in the fabric, raise the presser foot, pivot, and stitch across the bottom of the zipper just below the stay. When you get ¼in (5mm) beyond the opening edge, pivot again and stitch ¼in (5mm) from the opening edge. When you are back to the top mark, stop with the needle in, raise the presser foot, and open the zipper just enough to get the zipper pull out of the way. Repeat the pivoting procedure, and stitch across the top to your starting point.

5 Instead of backstitching, which is too noticeable when topstitching, leave long ends of thread at the beginning and end, and use a pin to pull the top threads through to the wrong side, then tie them and the bobbin threads together, and trim off the ends. Remove the hand basting, and use a seam ripper to remove the machine basting along the seam line over the zipper.

Covering buttons

For every covered button, you need a scrap of fabric plus a covered-button kit, which consists of a button form and a back plate. If your fabric is lightweight or sheer, use a double thickness or include an inside layer in a heavier or more opaque fabric. If you plan to cover a lot of buttons, I recommend buying a button-covering tool.

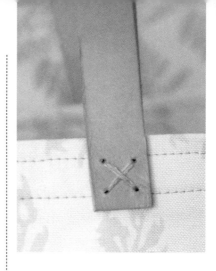

To cover a button without a specialist tool, cut out a circle of fabric slightly less than twice the diameter of the button form. Hand sew running stitch around the edge of the circle. Leaving the thread and needle attached to the fabric, place the button form, top side down, in the center of the fabric circle on the wrong side. Pull the thread to gather the fabric tightly around the button form. If there are tiny prongs inside the rim, press the fabric into them to hold it in place. Otherwise, use the needle and thread to make a few stitches from one side to the other, then tie the ends. Smooth out any bumps in the fabric, and press the back plate into position.

To use a button-covering tool, cut out a circle of the diameter specified in the tool's instructions. Place the fabric circle in the appropriately sized hole, wrong side up, and place the button form on this, top side down. Fold the fabric circle inward, tucking the raw edges inside the button form. Place the back plate on top and the corresponding part of the tool lid on top of that, raised side up. Press down on the tool lid to click the back plate into position, then remove the tool lid and pop out the covered button from the hole.

Attaching covered buttons

To sew on a covered button (or any button with a shank rather than holes in the button itself), thread the needle with a doubled length of thread, knot the ends, and fasten this on the right side of the fabric using two or three tiny stitches. Thread the button onto the needle and make about six stitches through the fabric and through the hole in the button shank. Fasten the thread on the wrong side with a few tiny stitches; on the last stitch, tie a small knot that sits against the fabric. Snip the thread close to the stitching.

Making and attaching leather handles

1 Use a craft knife or a rotary cutter, with a metal ruler and a cutting mat, to cut the leather strips to the desired length. If you wish, paint the edges using a small brush and acrylic paint, and leave to dry.

2 Mark four holes at each end of the handle, then lay it on a cutting mat and push a craft pick all the way through the leather at the marked points. Turn the handle over and insert the craft pick back into the holes from this side so they will be large enough to thread a needle through.

3 To attach the handle to the project, thread a needle with embroidery floss (thread) and tie a knot in the end of the floss. Insert the needle into the project from the inside, bringing the needle up through the bottom left hole of the handle, then inserting it through the top right hole; repeat two or three times more. Now bring the needle up through the top left hole, and insert it through the bottom right hole; repeat two or three times. In addition to this "X" shape, you can, if you wish, make stitches parallel and at right angles to the edges, to create a box around the "X." To finish, knot the floss on the wrong side and snip off the ends.

Material considerations

Fabrics

The projects in this book are mainly made from the following fabrics.

CANVAS For many projects in this book I used a canvas that is 55 percent linen and 45 percent cotton. Canvas differs from other heavy cotton fabrics in being a plain weave rather than a twill weave.

LINEN Some of the projects are made from a medium-weight 100 percent linen fabric with a soft finish.

LIGHTWEIGHT COTTON Many projects use lightweight cotton shirting fabric or quilting fabrics, embroidered cotton voile, or eyelet fabric (broderie anglaise).

OILCLOTH Once a cotton or linen coated with oil to make it waterproof. These days oilcloth is generally cotton or linen fabric with a vinyl (PVC) coating.

FELT I use 100 percent wool felt, as I like the look and feel of natural felt.

LININGS I use either 100 percent cotton or a lightweight linen-look polycotton.

Trimmings

These make all the difference between a plain project and something really appealing. All are available from notions (haberdashery) departments, craft shops, quilting and sewing shops, and online.

EYELET TRIM (BRODERIE ANGLAISE TRIM) I often use this polycotton trim, which incorporates embroidery, cutwork, and needle lace. This comes with one finished (scalloped) edge or two; use the former if the raw edge of the trim will be hidden.

CROCHET TRIM The loops on this cotton trim make great button loops. It is available in a host of colors, widths, and designs.

POMPOM TRIM This woven trim, with its decorative balls or tufts of fiber, looks good as an edging on pillows.

RICKRACK A flat, narrow braid woven in zigzag form, rickrack is usually sold by the yard (meter) and comes in loads of colors and sizes.

Invisibles

Though not visible, these behind-the-scenes materials fulfill important functions.

COTTON BATTING (WADDING) This is a sheet of cotton fibers that have been processed and wadded or "flattened." I've used it as padding for projects such as the Pieced Throw on page 64.

STUFFING For stuffing, I prefer 100 percent polyester high-loft fiberfill toy filling, as it is washable and safe.

FUSIBLE MATERIALS These are coated with a heat-activated adhesive that melts when heat and pressure are applied with an iron, bonding two layers together. Fusible interfacing, which has adhesive on one side, is fused to the wrong side of fabrics to strengthen and stabilize them. Fusible bonding web has adhesive on both sides and is used to fuse layers together. Before applying fusible materials, prewash the fabrics to remove the manufacturer's finishes, which could otherwise prevent a good bond. Methods of application vary, so follow the manufacturer's instructions.

Chapter 2

The Entrance Hall

The entrance hall is the first place you greet your guests. Whether yours is separated from the rest of your home or merges with the living room, the key to a well-designed entrance hall is ensuring that it is welcoming and clutter free. I have several hooks strung with an assortment of bags that work well as storage for scarves, hats, and other knickknacks that can clutter up a hall. If you have enough space to add a chair or a bench with soft pillows, then it will be comfortable as well as functional. With all this in mind, I have included in this chapter projects for stylish bags, a pretty patchwork pillow, and a floral brooch to adorn your coats, bags, or pillows.

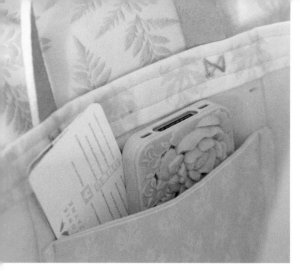

two-print bag

I often use this cute two-print bag as extra storage and hang it from a hook in my hallway, but I have been known to sneak it out and use it as a tote bag! There's a useful inside pocket for keys, tickets, or your phone. Decorate it with a felt rose brooch (see page 28) or hang a pretty lavender tag (see page 76) from one of the handles.

you will need

Pearlized acrylic paint and small paintbrush

Two 12½in (32cm) lengths of ¾in- (20mm-) wide bridle leather

One 7 x 10¼in (18 x 26cm) rectangle each of fabric A, lining, and medium-weight fusible interfacing for pocket

Matching sewing thread

Two 14¾ x 10½in (37 x 27cm) rectangles of fabric A, for bag bottom panel

Two 14¾ x 7⅞in (37 x 20cm) rectangles of fabric B, for bag top panel

One 14¾ x 34½in (37 x 88cm) rectangle of medium-weight fusible interfacing for bag

One 14¾ x 30in (37 x 76cm) rectangle of fabric C, for bag lining

Embroidery floss

dimensions

The finished bag measures 14 x 15in (35 x 38cm).

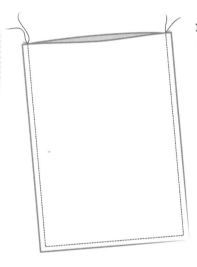

1 Paint the edges of the bridle-leather straps as shown in step 1 of Bag Storage, page 80, and leave to dry. Next make the pocket. Iron the small rectangle of interfacing to the wrong side of the pocket fabric A, following the manufacturer's instructions. With right sides together and raw edges even, pin the interfaced pocket to the pocket lining. Starting at the top, stitch a ⅜in (1cm) seam down one long edge, across the bottom, and up the other long edge to the top, pivoting the fabric at the bottom corners. Snip off the corners of the seam allowances.

2 Turn the pocket right side out and press. With the pocket face down on your work surface and the lining on top, fold up the bottom of the pocket by 4in (10cm). Pin along the side edges, then stitch a ⅜in (1cm) seam on each of the two side edges.

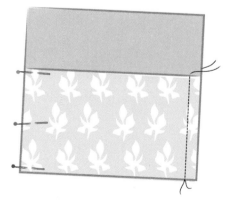

3 For the front, pin the lower edge of one top panel (fabric B) to the upper edge of one bottom panel (fabric A), with right sides together and raw edges even, making sure the pattern will face in the right direction after the pieces are stitched. Stitch a ³⁄₈in (1cm) seam, press the seam open, and then press the seam allowances toward the top panel. Repeat for the remaining top and bottom panels to make the back.

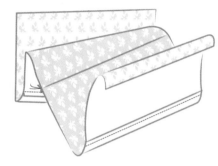

4 With right sides together and raw edges even, pin the front to the back, and stitch a ³⁄₈in (1cm) seam across the bottom edge only. Press the seam open.

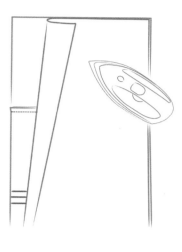

5 Following the manufacturer's instructions, iron the large rectangle of interfacing to the wrong side of the joined front and back. Topstitch ¼in (5mm) above the seam line joining the top and bottom panels on both the front and the back (not forgetting that the top of the back is currently at the lower edge of the large rectangle).

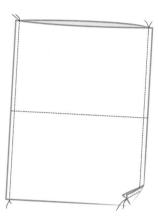

6 Fold the piece in half crosswise and pin the front to the back along both sides, with right sides together, aligning the seams joining the top and bottom panels. Stitch a ⅜in (1cm) seam on each side. Press the seams open, snipping into the fold of the interfacing seam allowances at the bottom of each seam so that they will open.

7 Make the lining by following step 6 for the lining rectangle (fabric C). Press 1¼in (3cm) and then a further 1¼in (3cm) to the wrong side around the upper edge of the outer bag; pin this double hem in place. With the outer bag right side out and the lining wrong side out, slip the lining inside the outer bag, so they are wrong sides together and the side seams are aligned. Tuck the upper edge of the lining under the hem; pin. Place the upper portion of the pocket from steps 1 and 2 centrally on top of the lining, tucking it under the hem too; pin. Starting at one side seam, topstitch the hem in place, ⅜in (1cm) from the top and then again ¾in (2cm) from the top.

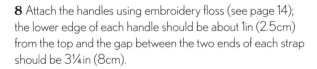

8 Attach the handles using embroidery floss (see page 14); the lower edge of each handle should be about 1in (2.5cm) from the top and the gap between the two ends of each strap should be 3¼in (8cm).

variation: tote bag

To make a large tote bag using the same basic method as for the Makeup Bag on page 110, cut the rectangles 14¾in (37cm) wide and 15¼in (39cm) tall and use a 14in (35cm) zipper. In step 1, after interfacing the print rectangles, pin and stitch a 14¾in (37cm) length of crochet trim across the right side of one piece, 3¾in (9.5cm) from the top edge; repeat for the other piece. At the end of step 6, tie a leather thong instead of rickrack to the zipper pull. Paint the edges of two 11½ x ⅝ x ⅛in (29cm x 16mm x 3mm) bridle-leather straps, leave to dry, and then attach one to each side with embroidery floss, as for steps 1 and 6 of the Bag Storage, pages 80–82.

patchwork pillow

There's nothing like patchwork for providing the opportunity to mix pretty prints in one project, and a pillow is an ideal way to try this craft, being small in scale but big on impact. If making buttonholes is not your thing, you will love how the back of this pillow buttons up—a strip of cotton crochet trim creates natural buttonholes that involve no work whatsoever.

you will need

Nine 6¾in (17cm) squares of cotton canvas in assorted prints

Matching sewing thread

One 18¾in (47cm) square of cotton batting (wadding)

Two rectangles of matching or coordinating fabric for the back, one 18¾ x 9¾in (47 x 25cm) and one 18¾ x 11¾in (47 x 29cm)

One 18¾in (47cm) length of crochet trim, with loops large enough for ³⁄₈in (10mm) buttons

Eight flower-shaped, four-hole, ³⁄₈in (10mm) buttons

One 18in (45cm) square pillow form (cushion pad)

dimensions

The finished pillow measures 18in (45cm) square.

Front

1 Start by laying out the nine squares into three rows of three squares each, and decide on the most attractive arrangement. Pin the first two squares from one row with their right sides together and raw edges even. Stitch a ³⁄₈in (1cm) seam down the side edge. Attach the third square to the middle one in the same way, forming the first row. Repeat to make two more rows. Press the seams open.

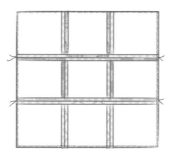

2 Pin the top two rows with right sides together and raw edges even, making sure that the seams align. Stitch a ³⁄₈in (1cm) seam. Repeat to join the bottom row to the middle row, forming your patchwork square. Press the seams open. Zigzag stitch the outer raw edges, so that they won't ravel when the cover is laundered.

3 Place the patchwork front, right side up, on top of the batting (wadding) square, and pin all over, then hand baste (tack) the two layers together and remove the pins. With the patchwork side on top, topstitch ¼in (5mm) on both sides of each seam line. Remove the basting.

TIP ROTARY CUTTERS For neat, straight, accurate lines when cutting out patches, use a rotary cutter and quilter's ruler with a cutting mat. These will be especially useful if you plan to do a lot of patchwork, as you can cut more than one layer at once. Always cut in a vertical line away from yourself, and keep your other hand well away from the cutter.

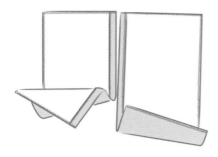

Back

4 On each back piece, zigzag stitch the raw edges and then turn under a ¾in (2cm) hem on one long edge. Press flat.

5 Pin the crochet trim to the underside of the smaller back piece along the pressed fold, making sure that it projects far enough beyond the edge to allow the loops to fit over the buttons you'll be attaching. Stitch the trim in place.

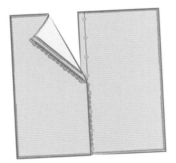

6 On the larger back piece, stitch the hem, and then place the smaller back piece on top, overlapping the hemmed edges by 1¼in (3cm) and with both pieces right side up. The distance between the side edges of the overlapping pieces should be 18¾in (47cm). Using pins, mark the position of buttons on the underneath (larger) back piece 1½in (4cm) away from its hemmed edge, in line with the loops on the crochet trim of the smaller back piece. Sew the buttons in place and button the two back pieces together.

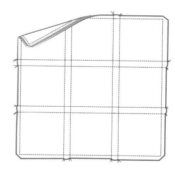

Joining front and back

7 Place the back on the front, with right sides together and raw edges even. Pin and then stitch a ⅜in (1cm) seam around the edge, pivoting the fabric at the corners. Clip the corners of the seam allowance. Trim away the batting within the seam allowance to make it less bulky. Unbutton the cover and turn it right side out. Use a blunt-ended tool, such as the rounded end of a chopstick, to carefully push out the corners. Press the cover, insert the pillow form (cushion pad), and button up the back.

oilcloth shopper

You can never have too many shopping bags! For this shopper, I used a softer cotton vinyl (PVC) fabric that has a wipe-clean finish. Because the front, base, and back are cut as one piece, you'll need to choose a fabric that looks good upside down. The long straps are made from herringbone tape adorned with grosgrain ribbon.

1 With right sides together and raw edges even, paperclip the top 13⅜in (34cm) of the left-hand long edge of the main piece to the right-hand long edge of one of the side pieces (see Tips about sewing on oilcloth, on page 129). Stitch a ⅜in (1cm) seam, stopping ⅜in (1cm) before the lower edge of the side piece. At the point where the stitching ends, snip into the seam allowance of the main piece at right angles to the stitching.

2 Pivoting the fabric around the corner, paperclip the middle 4in (10cm) of the left edge of the main piece to the bottom edge of the side piece, with right sides together and raw edges even. Stitch a ⅜in (1cm) seam, starting and stopping ⅜in (1cm) from the edges of the side piece. Snip into the seam allowance of the main piece, as in step 1.

3 Again pivoting the fabric around the corner, paperclip the remainder of the left edge of the main piece to the other long edge of the side piece, with right sides together and raw edges even. Starting at the top edge, stitch a ⅜in (1cm) seam, stopping ⅜in (1cm) from the bottom.

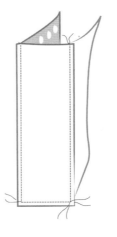

you will need

One 30¾ x 16¾in (78 x 42cm) rectangle of vinyl- (PVC-) coated cotton fabric, for main piece

Two 13¾ x 4¾in (35 x 12cm) rectangles of vinyl-coated cotton fabric, for side pieces

Teflon foot for sewing machine (see page 8)

Matching sewing thread

One 40¾ x 1½in (102 x 4cm) strip of vinyl-coated cotton fabric, for facing

Two 19in (48cm) lengths of ⅝in- (15mm-) wide fusible bonding web

Two 19in (48cm) lengths of ⅝in- (15mm-) wide grosgrain ribbon (with decorative stitching along edges, if desired)

Two 19in (48cm) lengths of 1in- (25mm-) wide cotton herringbone tape

Two 16 x 4in (40 x 10cm) rectangles of vinyl-coated cotton fabric, for base insert

One 16 x 4in (40 x 10cm) rectangle of stiff interfacing, for base insert

dimensions

The finished bag measures 16in (40cm) wide x 4in (10cm) deep x 13in (33cm) tall.

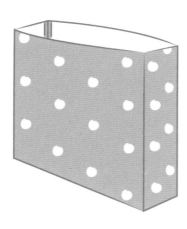

4 Repeat steps 1–3 to attach the other long edge of the main piece to the other side piece. Snip off the corners of the seam allowances, and turn right side out. Using a blunt-ended tool such as the rounded end of a chopstick, carefully push out the corners.

5 With right sides together and raw edges even, paperclip the short edges of the facing together, and stitch a ³⁄₈in (1cm) seam, forming a ring. Following the manufacturer's instructions, iron one side of the fusible bonding web to one grosgrain ribbon, and then the other side to one length of herringbone tape, to bond the ribbon down the center of the tape. Repeat for the other ribbon and tape.

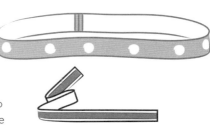

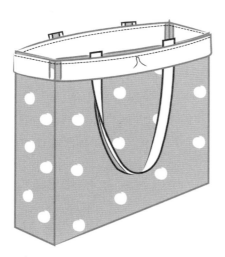

6 With raw edges even, paperclip the ends of one handle to the front of the bag at the top edge, 4¼in (11cm) from the side seams, with the ribbon side of the handle facing the right side of the bag. Paperclip the second handle to the back of the bag in the same way. Place the bag facing on top, right side down, with raw edges even, and with the seam even with one of the seams on the bag. The handles will be sandwiched between the facing and the bag. Stitch a ³⁄₈in (1cm) seam around the top.

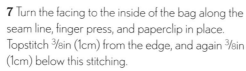

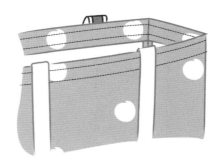

7 Turn the facing to the inside of the bag along the seam line, finger press, and paperclip in place. Topstitch ³⁄₈in (1cm) from the edge, and again ³⁄₈in (1cm) below this stitching.

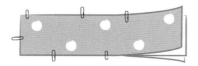

8 For the base insert, sandwich the rectangle of stiff interfacing between the two vinyl rectangles with wrong sides together and raw edges even; paperclip in place. Stitch them together ¼in (5mm) seam from the edges. Place inside the base of the bag.

variation: tall oilcloth shopper

This bag, which is 12in (30cm) wide x 5in (12cm) deep x 18in (45cm) tall, is made in much the same way, but using two vinyl fabrics for the main piece and sides. The main piece should be 43¼ x 12¾in (108 x 32cm) and the two side pieces should each be 19½ x 5¾in (49 x 14cm). The two vinyl and one stiff interfacing pieces should be 12 x 5in (30 x 12cm). Instead of tape/ribbon handles, each handle is made by edge stitching two 19½ x 1⅛in (49 x 2.7cm) strips (one of each fabric) with wrong sides together. Rather than having a facing, the top edge is simply turned down by 1⅛in (3cm) and topstitched with two rows of stitching. The ends of the handles are then stitched onto the outside, 1½in (4cm) from the top edge and 2¾in (7cm) from the side seams, stitching each as an "X" within a square (see page 133, step 8).
I also topstitched ⅜in (1cm) from the side seams, through both the main piece and the side piece, stopping ⅜in (1cm) from the bottom.

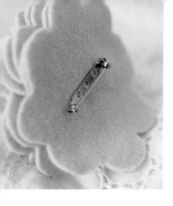

rose brooch

Surprisingly easy to do, this pretty felt rose makes a very stylish brooch. Very versatile, roses like this can also be used to adorn pillows or a handmade tote, strung together to make a garland, or turned into napkin holders (see pages 14, 18, 49, and 62).

(see pages 14, 18, 49, and 62).

you will need

One 8¼ x 12in (21 x 30cm) piece of felt

Matching sewing thread

1in (25mm) brooch pin

Hot-glue gun (optional)

1 Transfer the templates on page 139 onto your fabric using a water-soluble marker or a dressmaker's pencil; you will need five large rose pieces and two small rose pieces. Cut out the seven pieces.

2 Fold one large rose piece into quarters and place on top of another large rose piece, which will be the base. Position the folded piece with the folded corner at the center of the base, as shown. Hand sew in place by taking a few small stitches through the folded corner.

3 Fold a second large rose piece into quarters and place it on the base next to the first folded one, with the folded corner at the center of the base as shown. Hand sew in place, as in step 2. Repeat for a third large rose piece.

4 Add the remaining large rose piece to the base, so that you have four folded pieces arranged around the base piece; sew in place as in step 2.

5 Fold one of the small rose pieces into quarters and place on top of the large folded pieces. Hand sew in place as in step 2. Fold the remaining small rose piece into quarters and place it next to the previous one; hand sew in place.

6 Attach the brooch pin to the back of the felt rose by hand sewing it in place or using a hot-glue gun.

Chapter 3

The Kitchen and Dining Room

The kitchen and eating area are the heart of the home, so for this chapter I have designed projects that make everyday tasks more pleasurable while adding color and style to the kitchen and your dining table. There is a cook's apron, a pretty and practical oven mitt and a matching potholder, and trimmed tea towels, all of which can hang from hooks or pegs, making a lovely feature wall. There is also a stylish utensil holder, which is made in the same way as a bread bowl, and a bag made from linen to keep your bread fresh. To spruce up your dining table while adding comfort, I have designed buttoned pillows that are perfect on wooden chairs and can be flipped over to change the color emphasis in a jiffy. Finally, pretty napkins trimmed with crochet edging can be rolled up and slipped inside the accompanying floral napkin rings for special meals.

cook's apron

Choose two coordinating fabrics for this classic butcher's apron. The style is a perennial favorite with cooks, probably because it is long enough to provide adequate protection against splatters. The apron wraps around to the back, and the crossover straps don't put a strain on your neck. It can look pretty and feminine, or sharp and punchy, depending on the fabrics you use. Once you've made one, you'll find it easy to sew more in different fabrics or colors, to give to friends and family.

1 Using the patterns for the main piece and band on page 136, cut out one main piece from the canvas A square, one band from the canvas B rectangle, and one band from the fusible interfacing. With a water-soluble marker or a dressmaker's pencil, mark the pleat lines on the right side at the top edge of the main piece. Make a narrow inverted pleat as for step 3 of the Gardener's Apron, page 130, treating the central fold as the placement line, using pins rather than paperclips to secure the pleats on the top edge. Machine baste the pleat in place, ¼in (5mm) from the top edge.

2 Along the side and bottom edges, press ⅜in (1cm) and then a further ⅜in (1cm) hem to the wrong side. Stitch close to the inside fold all the way around this double hem. Use the crochet-edge bias tape (bias binding) to bind both curved armhole edges, as shown on page 12.

you will need

One 39in (1m) square of cotton canvas fabric A for main piece

One 11½ x 6in (29 x 15cm) rectangle of cotton canvas fabric B for band

One 11 x 5in (27 x 12cm) rectangle of fusible interfacing for band

One 12½ x 8in (32 x 20.5cm) rectangle of cotton canvas fabric B for pocket

Matching sewing thread

2¾yd (2.5m) of ⅜in- (10mm-) wide crochet-edge bias tape (bias binding)

One 12½in (32cm) length of ⅜in- (10mm-) wide cotton trim

Four grommets (eyelets) with ⅜in (10mm) holes

Two 59in (1.5m) lengths of 1in- (25mm-) wide cotton tape

Two ¾in (2cm) beads

dimensions

The finished apron is 35¾in (90.5cm) long and 33½in (85cm) wide excluding the straps.

3 Following the manufacturer's instructions, iron the interfacing to the wrong side of the band so that it is ³/₈in (1cm) in from the top and centered on the width. On the bottom edge of the band, press a double ³/₈in (1cm) hem to the wrong side, pin, and stitch, as in step 2. Center the band at the top of the main piece, with right sides together, the long raw edges even, and ³/₈in (1cm) projecting beyond each side edge of the main piece. Pin in place. Stitch a ³/₈in (1cm seam) along the long top edge. Flip the band up, away from the main piece, and press.

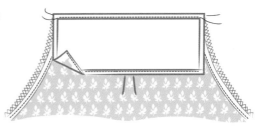

4 Fold the band in half, with right sides together, so that the hemmed edge just covers the seam; pin in place. Now stitch a ³/₈in (1cm) seam at each end of the band. Snip off the corners of the seam allowances.

5 Turn the band right side out, ensuring that the raw edges of the seams are tucked inside; pin in place. Topstitch the band ¼in (5mm) from the seam joining the band and the main piece.

6 On the top long edge of the pocket rectangle, press under 1¼in (3cm) and then a further 1¼in (3cm) to make a double hem; pin. Topstitch in place 1in (2.5cm) from the top folded edge. Pin the cotton trim to the wrong side of the hemmed edge, so that it projects beyond it. Stitch in place. Stitch another line ¼in (5mm) below this, starting and stopping just over ¼in (5mm) from the side edges of the pocket. Press under ³/₈in (1cm) on the remaining three edges.

7 Pin the wrong side of the pocket to the right side of the main piece, in the position shown on the pattern. Hand baste (tack) in place, then topstitch close to the edge down one side, across the bottom, and up the other side, pivoting the fabric at the corners. Repeat, stitching ¼in (5mm) inside the first stitching lines, starting and stopping at the middle row of horizontal stitching across the top. Remove the basting stitches.

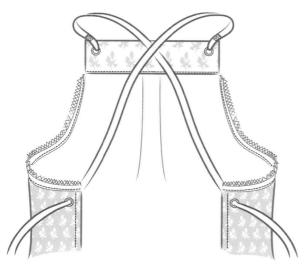

8 Mark the positions of the two grommets (eyelets) at either side of the top band and the two grommets on the main piece just under the armholes, as shown on the pattern. Following the manufacturer's instructions, insert the four grommets. Attach one end of each length of tape to a grommet at the top of the apron, as shown in step 8 of the Gardener's Apron, page 133. Thread the other end of each length of tape through the grommet beneath the opposite armhole, so that the straps cross at the back. Thread a bead onto each of these ends, and tie a knot in the tape to hold it in place.

double oven mitt

A double oven mitt is ideal for taking a heavy dish out of the oven with two hands, and making one that incorporates insulated batting (wadding) means that it will be just as protective as any you can buy. With its contrasting crochet trim it is also prettier, and you can choose fabrics to match your kitchen decor.

you will need

Two 8 x 7in (21 x 17cm) rectangles each of cotton canvas fabric A, cotton fabric for lining, and insulated batting (wadding)

One 35 x 7in (89 x 17cm) rectangle each of cotton canvas fabric A, cotton canvas fabric B, and insulated batting

Matching sewing thread

Basting spray (optional)

Two 7in (17cm) lengths each of bias tape (bias binding) and crochet trim for front

One 3½in (9cm) length of bias tape for loop

One 78in (2m) length of ½in- (15mm-) wide bias tape for outer edge

dimensions

The finished double oven mitt measures 6¾ x 35in (17cm x 89cm).

1 Using a water-soluble marker or a dressmaker's pencil, transfer the mitt template on page 138 to the two smaller canvas A rectangles, the two lining rectangles, and the two smaller batting (wadding) rectangles, and cut out the pieces. For one mitt, sandwich a piece of batting (wadding) between a canvas A piece and a lining piece, with the right side of the fabric pieces facing outward. Pin and then zigzag the layers together around the outside. Repeat for the second mitt.

2 Pin the crochet trim along the straight edge of one mitt on the canvas side; machine baste (tack) in place. Bind the straight edge as shown on page 12. Repeat for the second mitt.

3 Transfer the other template on page 138 to the two longer canvas rectangles and the longer batting rectangle, and cut out the pieces. On the right side of the canvas B piece, use the water-soluble marker or dressmaker's pencil to draw quilting lines, following the pattern on the fabric if you wish. Place this piece on top of the batting; pin and then baste (tack) or use basting spray. Machine stitch along the quilting lines, and remove the basting stitches if used.

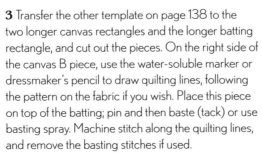

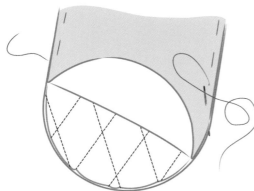

4 Place the remaining canvas piece against the batting side of the quilted piece, so that the right sides of the fabrics face outward. Baste or use the spray to hold the pieces together. Zigzag all around the edge.

5 Pin a mitt, right side up, at each end of the long piece, on the quilted side, with the edges even. Baste in place around the edge.

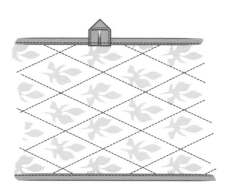

6 Make the small length of bias tape (bias binding) into a hanging loop, attach it to the quilted side at the center of one long edge, and bind the edges, as shown in steps 6 and 7 of the Pot Holder (page 40).

potholder

Keep your hands and worktops safe with this pretty yet practical potholder, which you can use either as a heatproof pad when taking things out of the oven or place under hot dishes to protect your work surface. Decorated with a contrasting crochet trim, it can be hung on a hook to make a stylish addition to your kitchen.

1 Using the template on page 138, round off all four corners of the squares and the two corners at one long edge of the rectangles. To quilt the base, use a water-soluble marker or a dressmaker's pencil to draw a series of quilting lines on the right side of one canvas square, adjusting them to follow the pattern of the fabric if you wish. Either hand baste (tack) or use basting spray to attach the batting (wadding) square to the wrong side of this fabric square. Machine stitch along the quilting lines, and remove the basting stitches if used.

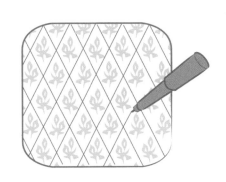

2 To complete the base, pin the other canvas square to the batting side of the quilted piece, with the right side facing outward. Machine baste a ¼in (5mm) seam all around the edge through all three layers.

3 For the front, sandwich the batting rectangle between the cotton canvas and cotton lining rectangles, with the right side of the fabric pieces facing outward. Pin and then machine baste around the edge, or use basting spray, to join the three layers together.

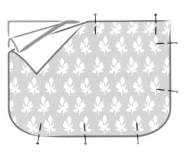

you will need

Two 8½in (22cm) squares of cotton canvas, for base

One 8½in (22cm) square of insulated batting (wadding), for base

One 8½ x 6¼in (22 x 16cm) rectangle each of cotton canvas, cotton fabric for lining, and insulated batting, for front

Basting spray (optional)

Matching sewing thread

One 44in (110cm) length of ½in- (15mm-) wide bias tape (bias binding)

One 9in (22cm) length of crochet trim

dimensions

The finished potholder measures 8½in (22cm) square.

4 Pin the crochet trim to the right side of the front along the top (straight) edge, and baste it in place. Using an 8½in (22cm) length of the bias tape (bias binding), bind this edge, as shown on page 12.

5 With both pieces right side up, lay the front on the base, aligning the bottom edges and the side edges; pin. Stitch a ⅜in (1cm) seam around the side and bottom edges of the front, through all layers. Now zigzag around the edge of the entire potholder.

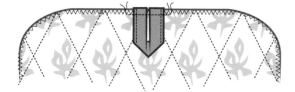

6 For the hanging loop, cut a 3¼in (9cm) length of the bias tape. Stitch the two sides of the tape together close to the edge. Now fold the tape as shown and place it at the center of the top edge of the potholder, with raw edges even. Stitch in place ¼in (5mm) from the raw edge.

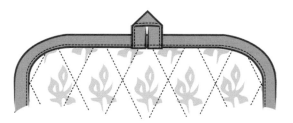

- -

TIP INSULATED BATTING This is made from hollow polyester fibers needle-punched through a reflective metalized polyester film, reflecting heat or cold back to its source. It is both breathable and washable, and is available from good craft stores or online.

- -

7 Use the remaining bias tape to bind the outer edges of the entire potholder, as shown on page 12, easing the binding around the curved corners, being careful not to stretch it. Pin the hanging loop in place so it is pointing upward before topstitching the front of the binding.

trimmed tea towels

With this easy sewing project, you'll wonder why you have never run up tea towels to match your kitchen decor before. Adding a useful grommet (eyelet) at one of the top corners allows you to hang the tea towel from a hook.

Crochet-trimmed tea towel

1 Press under ³⁄₈in (1cm) and then a further ³⁄₈in (1cm), forming a double hem, along the two long edges. Pin and then stitch in place. Repeat for the two short edges.

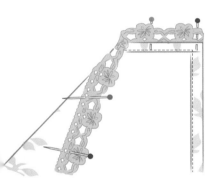

2 Apply fray-stop liquid to the cut ends of the two lengths of crochet trim; leave to dry. Pin one length of the trim to the right side of the tea towel along one short edge. Repeat for the other length and other short edge. Topstitch in place. Add a grommet (eyelet) to the top corner of the tea towel, following the manufacturer's instructions.

Bound-edge tea towel

1 Use the crochet-edge bias tape (bias binding) to bind the two shorter edges of the rectangle, as shown on page 12.

TIP FRAY-STOP LIQUID
This colorless liquid can be used to reinforce and bind textiles to prevent them from fraying.

2 On each long edge, press under ³⁄₈in (1cm) and then a further ³⁄₈in (1cm), forming a double hem. Pin and then stitch in place. Add a grommet (eyelet) to the top corner, following the manufacturer's instructions.

you will need

One rectangle of 100 percent cotton or linen fabric per tea towel, 18 x 21½in (46 x 54cm) for crochet-trimmed tea towel or 18 x 20in (46 x 50cm) for bound-edge tea towel

Matching sewing thread

Two 16½in (42cm) lengths of crochet trim, for crochet-trimmed tea towel

Two 18in (46cm) lengths of crochet-edge bias tape (bias binding), for bound-edge tea towel

Fray-stop liquid, for crochet-trimmed tea towel

Grommet (eyelet) kit

dimensions

Each finished tea towel measures 16½ x 20in (42 x 50cm), excluding the trim.

drawstring bread bag

Did you know that the best way to store your bread is in a fabric bag? This pretty linen drawstring bread bag keeps your bread fresher for longer, and looks pretty sitting on your kitchen counter or inside your pantry. If you don't have any crochet trim, you could use ribbon for the drawstring.

you will need

One 12¾ x 33in (32 x 84cm) rectangle of linen

Matching sewing thread

One 25in (64cm) length of ½in- (15mm-) wide bias tape (bias binding)

One 37in (94cm) length of crochet trim for drawstring

dimensions

The finished bag measures 12 x 16in (30 x 40cm).

1 Bind the two shorter sides of the linen rectangle, as shown on page 12. Fold the rectangle in half crosswise, right sides together, so the two bound edges are together at the top and the raw side edges are even. Pin down both sides. Starting at the bottom, stitch a ⅜in (1cm) seam on one side, stopping 1¼in (3cm) from the top. Stitch a seam of the same size on the other side, stitching all the way to the top this time. Snip off the corners of the seam allowances at the bottom and press the seams (including the unstitched section at the top) open.

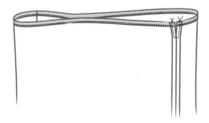

2 To hold in place the seam allowances of the seam that is open at the top, stitch from the top of one side down to where the side seam finishes, across to the other seam allowance and back up to the top.

3 To make the drawstring channel, turn under the top of the bag all the way around, wrong sides together, so that the edge of the binding lines up with the bottom of the open portion of the side seam. Press and pin all the way around to hold it in place. Stitch close to the edge of the binding around the top of the bag.

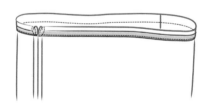

4 Turn the bag right side out and press. For the drawstring, attach a safety pin to one end of the crochet trim and feed it through the channel until it comes out the other side.

buttoned pillows

Make just one of these pillows or a whole set—they look great on wooden kitchen chairs or stools, and you can add interest with fabrics in two different colors for the front and back of each pillow, reversing the colors for the fabrics you use to cover the buttons.

you will need

One 16¾in (42cm) square each of two contrasting fabrics per pillow

Two 16¾in (42cm) squares of cotton batting (wadding) per pillow

Matching sewing thread

Basting spray (optional)

100 percent high-loft polyester toy filling

Eighteen ⅝in (15mm) covered buttons per pillow (see page 14)

Matte embroidery cotton and long upholstery needle

dimensions

The finished pillow measures 16in (40cm) square.

1 For the front, hand baste (tack) or use basting spray to attach a square of batting (wadding) to the wrong side of one fabric square. Zigzag around the edges. Using a water-soluble pen or a dressmaker's pencil, mark on the right side of the fabric where your buttons will go, spacing them 4in (10cm) from the edges and 4in (10cm) apart. Repeat with the other fabric square and batting square for the back of the pillow, making sure that the marks for the buttons are in exactly the same places as on the front.

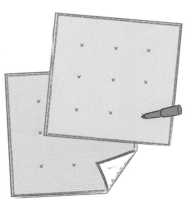

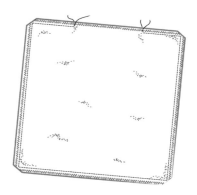

2 Pin the front to the back, with right sides together and raw edges even. Stitch a ⅜in (1cm) seam around all four edges, leaving an opening at the top edge. Snip off the corners of the seam allowances. Press the seam open.

3 Turn right side out through the opening, push out the corners, and then stuff the pillow, as in step 4 of the Garden Kneeler, page 129, until you have a firm, plump pillow.

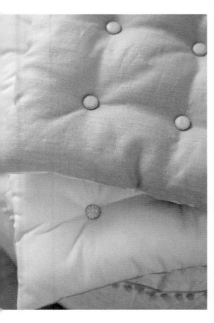

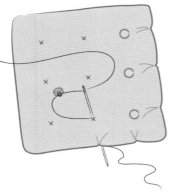

4 Thread a long upholstery needle with embroidery cotton, and button-tuft the pillow as in step 7 of the Padded Headboard, page 97. If necessary, add a little more stuffing to get the right shape and firmness. Remove the basting stitches if used. Fold in the seam allowances on the opening, and slipstitch closed.

napkin and ring

These crochet-trimmed napkins are great for everyday dining, or for more formal occasions you can dress them up with a felt rose napkin holder. Make a matching set, or use remnants of coordinating fabrics. Scale up the napkins to make pretty table mats or tablecloths with a professional finish.

you will need

for the napkin

One 18in (46cm) square of fabric for each napkin

Matching sewing thread

66in (168cm) crochet trim for each napkin

dimensions

The finished napkin measures 16½in (42cm).

for the napkin ring

Two 5½ x ¾in (14 x 2cm) strips each of felt and lightweight fusible interfacing per ring

Two 5in (12cm) leather thongs per ring

Matching sewing thread

Hot-glue gun (optional)

One felt rose (see page 28) per ring

Crochet-trimmed napkin

1 First you need to press a double hem all around the napkin. To do this, place the square of fabric wrong side up on your ironing board, fold over one edge to the wrong side by ⅜in (1cm), and press. Fold over and press the adjacent edge in the same way, and continue till all four edges are pressed to the wrong side. Going back to the first edge, fold it over again by another ⅜in (1cm), and press. Repeat around the napkin until all four edges are pressed to the wrong side a second time.

2 Now unfold the second round of hems but leave the first hems folded up, while you make machine-stitched miters on each corner. Fold the napkin diagonally with right sides together, lining up the adjacent folded edges of the napkin at one corner and also lining up the inner press lines. Pin in place. Align the long edge of a ruler with the diagonal fold of the napkin, and the corner of the ruler with the point where the inner press lines meet. Draw a line along the end of the ruler.

3 Machine stitch along the drawn line. Trim off the excess, leaving seam allowances of ¼in (5mm). Also snip off the corner of the seam allowance on the fold. Press the seam open.

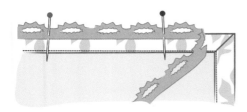

4 Repeat steps 2 and 3 to miter the other three corners. Fold the hems back into place along the pressed lines, carefully pushing out the corners. Press, pin, and then stitch around all four edges close to the inner fold, pivoting the fabric at each corner. Pin the crochet trim around the edge of the napkin, on the underside, so that it sits under the double hem and projects beyond the edge. Stitch in place, pivoting the fabric at each corner.

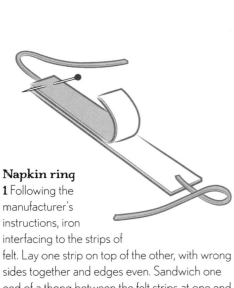

Napkin ring

1 Following the manufacturer's instructions, iron interfacing to the strips of felt. Lay one strip on top of the other, with wrong sides together and edges even. Sandwich one end of a thong between the felt strips at one end, overlapping it by 3/8in (1cm), and pin in place. Repeat for the other thong at the other end.

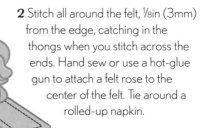

2 Stitch all around the felt, 1/8in (3mm) from the edge, catching in the thongs when you stitch across the ends. Hand sew or use a hot-glue gun to attach a felt rose to the center of the felt. Tie around a rolled-up napkin.

utensil pot

This stylish utensil pot will look great in your kitchen. It is also very versatile —adding a grommet (eyelet) at the back would allow you to hang it from a hook, or you could alter the size and put a jar or a can inside to add structure so you could use it for cutlery or craft tools. See page 53 for instructions for making the scaled-up bread bowl seen on the right.

1 On a piece of paper, draw a circle 4⅛in (10.5cm) in diameter. Measure the circle's circumference; it will be about 13in (33cm). Draw a rectangle with a length exactly equal to the circle's circumference, and with a width of 7in (18cm). Transfer these two patterns onto the wrong side of your linen square and rectangle, using a water-soluble marker or a dressmaker's pencil, with one long edge of the rectangle on the selvage. Repeat for the print fabric, again having one long edge on the selvage, and for the interfacing. Cut out all the pieces. Following the manufacturer's instructions, iron the interfacing circle and rectangle to the wrong side of the linen circle and rectangle.

you will need

One 5in (13cm) square each of linen, print lining fabric, and heavyweight fusible interfacing

One 8 x 14in (20.5 x 35.5cm) rectangle each of linen, print lining fabric, and heavyweight fusible interfacing, with one long edge of linen and of print fabric cut on selvage

Matching sewing thread

Pearlized acrylic paint and small paintbrush

Fusible bonding web (optional)

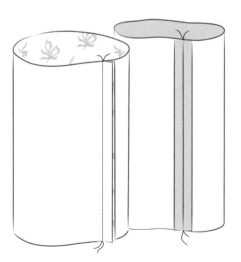

2 With right sides together, pin the short edges of the linen rectangle together, forming a cylinder shape. Stitch a ⅜in (1cm) seam and press the seam open. Repeat for the print fabric.

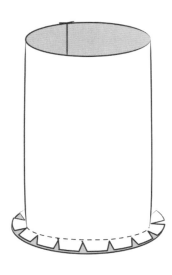

3 Staystitch (see page 9) around the lower (non-selvage) edge of the cylinder ⅜in (1cm) from the edge, and then make snips almost up to the staystitching. With the selvage edge at the top, stand the linen cylinder, wrong side out, on the right-side-up linen circle. The snips in the seam allowance will allow it to sit flat on the circle, as shown. With raw edges even, pin the lower edge of the cylinder to the circle around the edge.

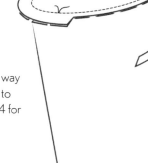

4 Stitch a ⅜in (1cm) seam all the way around. Trim the seam allowance to ¼in (5mm). Repeat steps 3 and 4 for the print fabric.

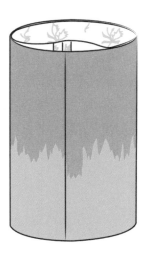

5 Turn the linen cylinder right side out and paint the base and part of the sides with acrylic paint; leave to dry. Slip the print-fabric cylinder, wrong side out, inside the right-side-out linen cylinder, so that the wrong sides are together. Line up the vertical seam lines.

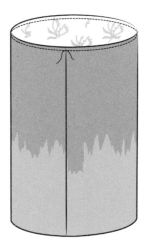

6 Either pin around the top and stitch ¼in (5mm) from this edge, or use fusible web (see page 15) to join the lining to the linen at the top. Now fold over the top of the pot once or twice to show off the lining.

variation: bread bowl

To make this stylish bread bowl, draw a larger circle and a rectangle with a shorter height; the one shown here is made from a circle 9in (23cm) in diameter and a rectangle 5in (13cm) high. The rectangles do not have to be cut on the selvage. Make the pot as in steps 1–5, but then bind the top edges of the linen and lining together with bias tape (bias binding), as shown on page 12.

Chapter 4

The Living Room

Successful decorating is the artful blending of colors, patterns, and textures to create a harmonious effect in the home. The easiest way to add warmth and character to your living room is with a selection of pillows and throws. In this chapter you will find a wide range of designer-look handmade designs, whether you are a beginner looking for a simple pillow project or an experienced sewer wanting a challenge. The pillows come in a variety of shapes, sizes, and fabrics, to add interest to your living room—and in the warmer months, you can take them outside, to have the same effect on your patio or in your garden. Finally, there is patchwork, in the form of an heirloom-quality throw and a wonderful ottoman pouf.

patchwork ottoman pouf

I love ottoman poufs and have several in my house, as they make great footrests and occasional seating. The style is inspired by Moroccan leather ottoman poufs. The one shown here is made from 35 different prints and is adorned with pompom trim and square sequins. It has an oilcloth base, which means you can even use it outside.

you will need

Cotton canvas scraps for top and sides

Matching sewing thread

One 21in (53cm) square and one 8in (20cm) square of fusible interfacing

One 24in (60cm) length of ½in- (15mm-) wide bias tape (bias binding)

Sequins (optional)

One 21in (53cm) square of cotton batting (wadding)

Basting spray (optional)

1¾yd (1.6m) of pompom trim

One 64 x 9in (163 x 23cm) rectangle of fusible interfacing

One 22½in (57cm) square of oilcloth, for base

One 19in (48cm) zipper in color to match oilcloth

Washi tape (see Tip)

One ottoman pouf pillow form (cushion pad) 20in (51cm) in diameter and 8in (20cm) high

dimensions

The finished pouf measures 20in (51cm) in diameter and 8in (20cm) high.

Top

1 Using a water-soluble marker or a dressmaker's pencil, transfer the wedge template on page 139 to the wrong side of your fabric scraps, and cut out 16 wedges. Arrange them in a ring, experimenting with the sequence until you are happy with it. Pin them in pairs along the long edges, with right sides together, and stitch ⅜in (1cm) seams. Now stitch the pairs together in the same way, and continue in this way until all the wedges are stitched into a ring. Press the seams open and snip off the corners of the seam allowances.

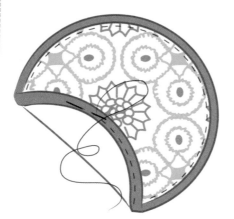

2 Transfer the circle template on page 139 to the wrong side of a fabric scrap and also to the smaller square of interfacing—you will need one of each. Cut out both circles. Following the manufacturer's instructions, iron the interfacing to the back of the circle. Now bind the edge of the interfaced circle, as shown on page 12, but hand baste (tack) rather than topstitching the second edge of the binding in place. Sew on any sequins or other embellishments to the circle.

TIP WASHI TAPE This decorative masking tape, which originated in Japan, is made from natural fibers and is surprisingly strong. I use it because it is easy to remove and reapply without leaving a residue.

3 With the patchwork ring right side up, place the bound circle, also right side up, on top of the ring, with the circle's outer edge overlapping the ring's inner edge. Pin and baste in place, then topstitch the central circle to the patchwork ring around the edge of the binding. Remove the basting stitches. Following the manufacturer's instructions, iron fusible interfacing to the wrong side of the entire patchwork top.

4 Draw around the edge of the interfaced top onto the batting (wadding) using a water-soluble pen. Hand baste or use basting spray to attach the batting to the wrong side of the patchwork top. Stitch around the central circle to create a quilted effect and machine stitch ¼in (5mm) from the outside edge of the top. Pin the pompom trim to the right side of the patchwork top just under ³⁄₈in (1cm) in from the outside edge, with the pompoms facing inward. Stitch in place ³⁄₈in (1cm) from the edge.

Sides

5 Transfer the side-piece template on page 139 to the wrong side of your fabric scraps, and cut out 16 rectangles. Experiment with their arrangement, and then pin them together along the long edges, right sides together, until you have one long strip. Stitch ³⁄₈in (1cm) seams, starting and stopping ³⁄₈in (1cm) from the ends. Press the seams open. Iron fusible interfacing to the wrong side of this strip, trimming it to fit. Snip into the top and bottom edges of the interfacing where the seams are unstitched. Pin the two ends of the strip with right sides together, and stitch a ³⁄₈in (1cm) seam, starting and stopping ³⁄₈in (1cm) from the ends. Press open.

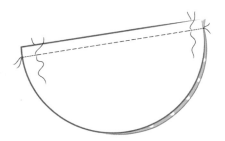

Base

6 Fold the patchwork top in half and lay it on the wrong side of the oilcloth. Draw around the edges, adding a ¾in (2cm) seam allowance to the straight edge; cut out. Place these two semicircles with right sides together, aligning the straight edge, and secure with paperclips, not pins (see Tips on page 129). Stitch a ¾in (2cm) seam along the straight edge, machine basting the central 19in (48cm) portion, as explained for step 2 of Applying a Zipper on page 13. Finger press the seam open rather than pressing it with an iron.

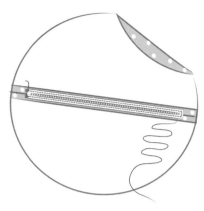

7 Apply the zipper as shown on page 13, but using a few strips of washi tape to hold it in place instead of pinning and hand basting it. After stitching it, remove the tape and the basting stitches holding the seam together.

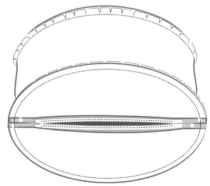

Assembly

8 With right sides together and raw edges even, pin the top to the upper edge of the sides, matching the seams. Ease or slightly stretch the fabric and make additional snips into the seam allowance on the upper edge of the sides as necessary. Stitch a 3/8in (1cm) seam. Open the zipper. With right sides together and raw edges even, join the base to the lower edge of the sides in the same way as for the top, but using paperclips rather than pins. Turn right side out, insert the pillow form (cushion pad), and close the zipper.

bolster

Bolsters are long, narrow pillows, which provide both comfort and style for your home and are great for daybed ends, for back support in bed, and at the ends of sofas and benches with arms. I also like to use mine at the ends of my garden bench.

you will need

One 22in (55cm) length of pompom trim

Two 7¾in (19cm) circles of fabric

One 18¾ x 25¾in (47 x 62.5cm) rectangle of fabric

One 18¾in (47cm) length of crochet trim, with loops that will fit ³⁄₈in (10mm) buttons

Three ³⁄₈in (10mm) buttons

Embroidery floss (thread) in contrasting color

One 18 x 7in (45 x 17cm) bolster form (cushion pad)

dimensions

The finished bolster measures 18in (45cm) in length and 7in (17cm) in diameter.

1 Pin the pompom trim around the edge of one fabric circle (starting at the base of the circle if your print is one-way), with the pompoms facing inward. Stitch in place ³⁄₈in (1cm) from the edge.

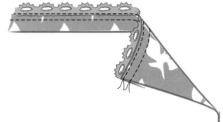

2 Turn under a 1¼in (3cm) hem on one short edge of the fabric rectangle; press and pin. Stitch ³⁄₈in (1cm) from the fold. Repeat for the other short edge. Pin the crochet trim along the underside of one hemmed edge, with the crochet loops projecting beyond the edge. Stitch the trim in place.

3 Staystitch (see page 9) just under ³⁄₈in (1cm) from the edge along both raw edges of the rectangle, starting and stopping at the hems. Snip almost up to the staystitching at 1in (2.5cm) intervals. Fold the rectangle into a cylinder, wrong side out, overlapping the hems, so that the edge that has the crochet trim is underneath, with the raw edge of the crochet trim even with the raw edge of the hem overlapping it. Pin in place at each end, and then machine baste the overlapping portions together ³⁄₈in (1cm) from the edge at each end.

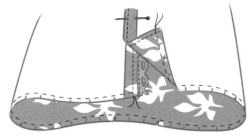

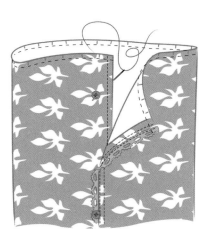

4 Turn the cylinder right side out and use pins to mark the positions of the three buttons on the underlapping portion, 1¼in (3cm) in from the hemmed edge—one should be in the center and one on each side of it, roughly 5½in (14cm) away, but each button also needs to be in line with a crochet loop. Sew on the buttons using embroidery floss, then turn the cylinder wrong side out again.

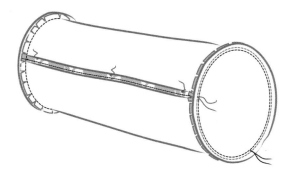

5 With right sides together, pin a fabric circle to one end of the cylinder, lining up the seam line with the point at which your pompom trim started and finished. The snips you made in the edge will open up to allow it to fit around the curve. With the circle on the bottom, stitch a ³⁄₈in (1cm) seam around the circle. Repeat at the other end of the cylinder, making sure the print is facing in the same direction, if applicable. Turn the cover right side out, insert the bolster form (cushion pad), and fasten the buttons.

basketweave pillow

This elegant pillow looks much more complicated than it actually is. Just remember to keep your woven lines straight. I used a dainty, softly colored eyelet (broderie anglaise) trim but you could substitute vibrant tartan ribbon or subtle twill tape for completely different effects.

you will need

One 16¾ x 10¾in (42 x 27cm) rectangle of fusible interfacing

Seventeen 10¾in (27cm) lengths and eleven 16¾in (42cm) lengths of 1in- (25mm-) wide eyelet (broderie anglaise) trim with two finished edges

Matching sewing thread

Two 16¾ x 8in (42 x 20cm) rectangles of fabric, for back

One 16¾in (42cm) length of narrow rickrack

1½yd (1.3m) of pompom trim

One 16 x 10in (40 x 25cm) pillow form (cushion pad)

dimensions

The finished pillow measures 16 x 10in (40 x 25cm).

1 Place the rectangle of fusible interfacing, adhesive side up, on your ironing board, with one of the long edges at the top. Starting at the top left corner, pin one of the short lengths of eyelet (broderie anglaise) trim along the left edge of the interfacing, pinning it at the top and bottom edges. Now place additional short lengths of trim butting up to each other, until you have pinned all 17 vertical lengths of trim across the interfacing.

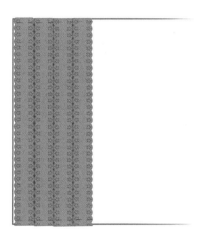

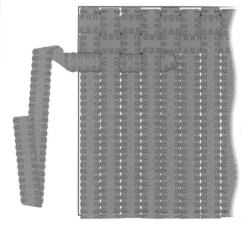

2 Starting at the top left corner of the interfacing, weave one of the long strips of trim horizontally through the vertical strips, alternately over and under, keeping the upper edge of the trim even with the top edge of the interfacing. Pin the ends in place at the ends, so that they are even with the side edges. Now weave a second long length of trim through the vertical lengths, butting it up to the previous horizontal one, and going over the vertical length when the previous horizontal length went under, and vice versa. Pin at both ends, as before. Weave the remaining long lengths in the same way, until all 11 horizontal lengths are woven in.

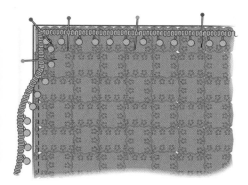

3 Place a pressing cloth over the woven trim and, following the manufacturer's instructions, iron it to the interfacing. Carefully machine baste all around, ¼in (5mm) from the edges. Now pin the pompom trim to the right side of the woven front just under ³⁄₈in (1cm) from the edge, with the pompoms facing toward the center. Stitch in place ³⁄₈in (1cm) from the edge.

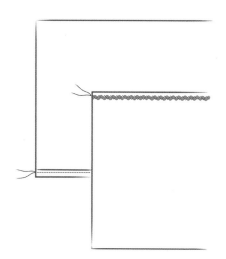

4 On one long edge of each back piece, press in a ³⁄₈in (1cm) double hem. Pin and stitch ⅛in (3mm) from the inner fold. On the right side of one back piece, pin a length of rickrack over the stitching line of the hem; zigzag in place. Complete the pillow as for steps 3 and 4 of the Pompom Pillow, page 102.

pieced throw

Delicate and feminine, this beautiful patchwork throw is destined to become a family heirloom. Because translucent fabrics and eyelet (broderie anglaise) fabric are used for the piecing, the front panel is lined, adding to the soft, ethereal effect.

1 Using pinking shears, cut out eighty-four 6in (15cm) squares from the assorted fabrics. Lay out the squares in twelve rows of seven squares each, and play around with their arrangement. Once you are happy with this, pin the first row of squares together at the side edges, with right sides together and raw edges even. Stitch ³⁄₈in (1cm) seams, and press the seams open. Repeat to join the squares in each of the remaining rows.

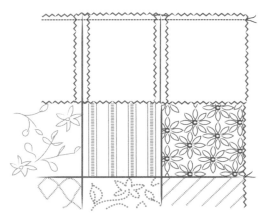

2 Pin the lower edge of the top row to the upper edge of the second row with right sides together, raw edges even, and seams matching. Stitch a ³⁄₈in (1cm) seam. Repeat to join the third row to the second, and continue in this way till all twelve rows are joined. Press the seams open. The patchwork panel should be 37½ x 63¾in (93 x 158cm) at this stage.

you will need

Pinking shears

Assorted cotton voiles, embroidered fabrics, and eyelet (broderie anglaise) fabric

Matching sewing thread

Two 72¼ x 5in (180 x 13cm) strips of cotton voile, for top and bottom borders

Two 46 x 5in (115 x 13cm) strips of cotton voile, for side borders

Two 72¼ x 46in (180 x 115cm) rectangles of matching or coordinating fabric, for front lining and back

6²⁄₃yd (6m) of eyelet trim (broderie anglaise trim) with one finished edge

Basting spray

One 72¼ x 46in (180 x 115cm) rectangle of batting (wadding)

Appliqué flowers (optional)

dimensions

The finished throw measures 71½ x 45¼in (178 x 113cm).

3 With right sides together and raw edges even, pin one of the longer border strips to one of the long edges of the patchwork panel (with equal amounts extending beyond the panel at each end). Stitch a ³/₈in (1cm) seam, starting and stopping ³/₈in (1cm) from the adjacent edge of the patchwork panel. Repeat to attach the other strip of the same length to the other long edge of the panel. Now attach the remaining two strips to the short edges of the panel in the same way, pushing the loose end of each adjacent strip out of the way as you go.

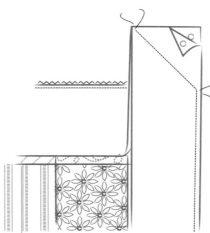

4 At each corner, miter the loose ends of the two strips that meet there by folding them separately on a diagonal line running between the inner and outer corners; finger press each to form a crease. Unfold, and, lining up the crease lines, pin the loose ends with right sides together along the aligned creases. Stitch along this line through the loose ends only. Trim off the excess, ³/₈in (1cm) outside the seam line. Press.

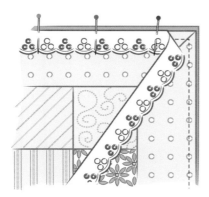

5 Place the patchwork panel on top of the lining, with the right sides of both facing upward and the raw edges even. Pin and machine baste all around, ¼ in (5mm) from each edge. Pin the eyelet (broderie anglaise) trim around the edges of the patchwork panel, with right sides together and aligning the straight edge of the trim with the raw edge of the panel. Stitch a ⅜in (1cm) seam all around, easing in a little extra trim at each corner so it will fit around the corner when turned right side out, and also clipping into the seam allowance at each corner to allow you to turn the corner when stitching.

6 Spray the wrong side of the back panel with basting spray and lay the batting (wadding) on it, smoothing out any creases. Machine baste all around, ¼ in (5mm) from the edges. With right sides together, pin the back to the front, with the trim sandwiched between them. Stitch a ⅜in (1cm) seam, starting in the center of one of the short sides, pivoting the fabric at the corners, and stopping 10in (25cm) from your starting point.

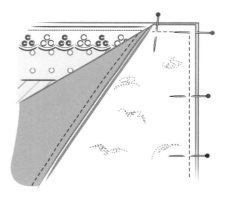

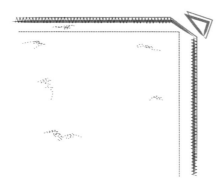

7 Snip off the corners of the seam allowances, and zigzag the raw edges. Turn right side out through the opening, and use a blunt tool such as the rounded end of a chopstick to push out the corners. Press. Turn in the seam allowances of the opening and slipstitch closed. Topstitch all around the throw, ⅜in (1cm) from the edge.

8 Hand baste (tack) the layers together at frequent intervals. Quilt the throw by topstitching ¼ in (5mm) each side of every seam. You can do this by machine (using a quilting foot on the machine—see page 8) or by hand, using running stitch and being careful to stitch through all layers. Remove the basting stitches. If you wish, hand sew appliqués to some of the plainer squares.

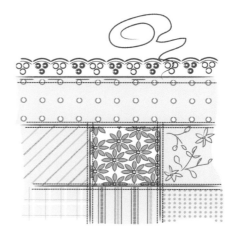

felt flower pillow

This unusual three-dimensional felt flower pillow has no less than 115 semicircular felt "petals." In three different sizes, they are machine stitched in circles around the front of the round pillow, with the largest petals on the outside and the smallest ones at the center.

you will need

One 12¾in (32cm) circle of felt for front of pillow

One 13 x 16in (33 x 40cm) rectangle of felt

One 37¾ x 2¼in (96.3 x 6cm) strip of felt for gusset

Lightweight interfacing for front, backs, and gusset

Thirty-eight 3in (7.5cm) circles of felt, cut in half

Ten 2½in (6.5cm) circles of felt, cut in half

Ten 1¾in (4.5cm) circles of felt, cut in half

Matching sewing thread

One 9in (23cm) zipper

One 12in (30cm) round pillow form (cushion pad)

dimensions

The finished pillow measures 12in (30cm) in diameter and 1½in (4cm) thick.

1 Make a pattern for the two back pieces by drawing around the 12½in (32cm) felt circle on paper. Fold this in half and cut along the crease. Now fold the felt rectangle in half crosswise and draw around one paper semicircle on the felt, but add a further ¾in (2cm) at the straight edge. Cut out the two pieces.

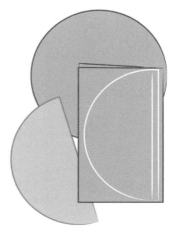

2 Interface the front, back, and gusset pieces. On the right side of the interfaced front, use a water-soluble marker or a dressmaker's pencil to mark concentric circles with diameters of 10¼in (26cm), 9in (23cm), 8in (20cm), 6¾in (17cm), 5in (13cm), 3¾in (9.5cm), and 2¼in (6cm).

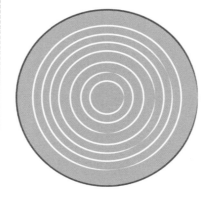

3 Pin 16 of the 3in (7.5cm) semicircles around the outer marked circle, with the pieces overlapping by roughly ¾in (2cm); stitch in place ¼in (5mm) from the straight edge.

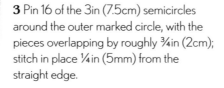

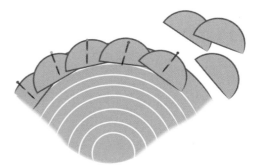

4 Repeat step 3 to attach 16 more of the same-size semicircles around the next marked circle, this time overlapping them by roughly 1in (2.5cm) and staggering them relative to the previous row. Repeat step 3 again to attach a further 16 of the same-size semicircles around the third marked circle, overlapping these by about 1¼in (3cm). Repeat step 3 again to attach 14 of the same-size semicircles around the fourth circle, overlapping them by about 1⅜in (3.5cm), and stitching just ⅛in (3mm) from the edge. Repeat step 3 to attach 13 semicircles of this size around the fifth circle, overlapping them by about 1½in (4cm) and again stitching ⅛in (3mm) from the edge. Discard the one remaining semicircle.

TIP GOING AROUND IN CIRCLES For this project you need to draw a lot of circles in three different sizes plus a fourth size for the front, and you may prefer to search for plates, cups, and glasses to draw around. However, the simplest way of ensuring the circles are exactly the right size is to use a compass and pencil to make paper patterns.

5 Pin 13 of the 2½in (6.5cm) semicircles around the sixth marked circle, with the pieces overlapping by roughly 1½in (4cm). Stitch ⅛in (3mm) from the straight edge. Repeat to attach 7 more of the same-size semicircles around the seventh (inner) marked circle, but with the pieces overlapping by roughly 1¼in (3cm).

6 Pin the 20 remaining small semicircles together as shown, overlapping them to form a long strip with the straight edges even. Stitch ¼in (5mm) from the straight edge.

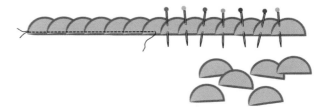

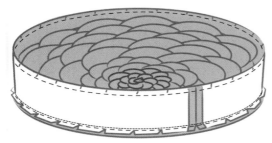

7 Roll up the strip into a spiral, and hand sew to the center of the pillow front, covering the remaining space.

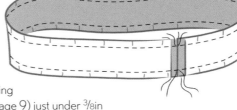

8 Pin the two short ends of the gusset with right side together and raw edges even; stitch a ³⁄₈in (1cm) seam, starting and stopping ³⁄₈in (1cm) from the edge. Press the seam open. Staystitch (see page 9) just under ³⁄₈in (1cm) from both edges, then clip into the seam allowance every 1¼–1½in (3-4cm).

9 Pin the gusset to the front, with right sides together and raw edges even, easing or slightly stretching as necessary. The snips in the seam allowances will open up to allow the gusset edge to sit flat on it. Stitch a ³⁄₈in (1cm) seam, sewing a few stitches at a time, then stopping with the needle down to adjust the fabric so that the round edge is always flat and not distorted. Keep doing this every few stitches.

10 Pin the back pieces together along the straight edge, with right sides together and raw edges even. Stitch a ¾in (2cm) seam, stitching for 1¾in (4.5cm) at each end and machine basting in between, and then apply the zipper, all as shown on page 13. Open the zipper and attach the other edge of the gusset strip to the back of the pillow, as you did for the front in step 9. Turn the pillow right side out, insert the pillow form (cushion pad), and close the zipper.

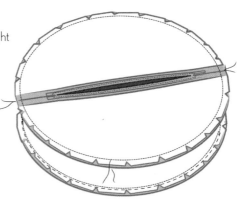

Chapter 5

The Laundry Room

The laundry room or space doesn't have to be boring—all you need are a few homemade sewing projects to quickly create an environment that will bring a smile to the face of anyone doing the laundry or ironing. With carefully selected fabrics, you can create a laundry area that either harmonizes with your kitchen or has a totally new look. In this chapter you will find the essentials, such as an ironing board cover, a linen basket, and bag storage, as well as coat hanger covers that supply bright pops of color and print, lavender tags that add a lovely aroma, and storage cubes that can be used all over your home to keep the clutter at bay. With a few tweaks to the linen basket project, you can also create a stylish basket to keep clothespins in.

coat hanger cover

These make lovely gifts and are ideal for hanging up your favorite clothes or brightening up your laundry room. The instructions include padding, which is useful for protecting the shoulders of jackets and dresses, but it can be omitted if you prefer. See page 76 for how to make the decorative tags hanging from the hooks.

1 For each cover, place the coat hanger on the wrong side of your fabric, and draw around the outside of the hanger, excluding the hook, adding a 3/8in (1cm) seam allowance all around the sides and top, and adding 3in (7.5cm) at the bottom. Carefully cut out two pieces of fabric and two pieces of batting (wadding).

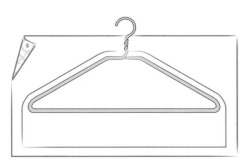

you will need

Wire coat hanger

Two 18 x 20in (45 x 25cm) rectangles each of fabric and cotton batting (wadding) per coat hanger

Matching sewing thread

One 34in (85cm) length of bias tape (bias binding) per coat hanger

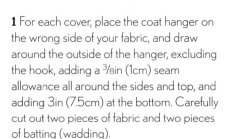

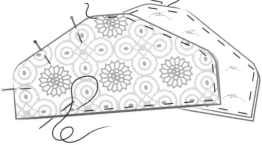

2 Pin each fabric piece right side up to one piece of batting. Baste (tack) together 1/4in (5mm) from the edge.

3 Pin the two padded pieces with right sides together and raw edges even. Stitch a 3/8in (1cm) seam all around the sides and top, leaving a gap at the center of the top for the coat hanger hook. Do not stitch across the bottom. Snip off the corners of the seam allowance and remove the basting stitches.

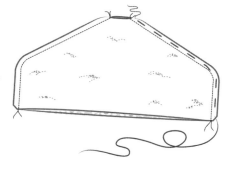

4 Turn the cover right side out and, using a blunt-ended tool such as the rounded end of a chopstick, carefully push out the corners. Bind the front hem and back hem continuously using the bias tape (bias binding), as shown on page 12. Insert the coat hanger into the cover from the bottom, and push the hook through the opening at the top.

lavender tags

These sweet lavender bags shaped like luggage tags will impart a pleasant scent wherever they are used. They make a delightful home decoration or a pretty gift. Loop them over clothes hangers in the closet or decorate door knobs or drawer handles with them.

1 Using a water-soluble marker or a dressmaker's pencil, transfer the template on page 137 onto the wrong side of your fabric; you will need two pieces for each tag. If you are using felt, omit the ¼in (5mm) seam allowance all around. Cut out the pieces. Pin two fabric pieces with right sides together; for felt, pin the two pieces with wrong sides together.

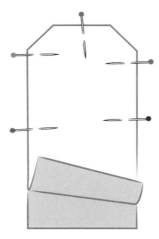

you will need

Scraps of fabric or felt

Matching sewing thread

One ¼in (5mm) grommet (eyelet) per tag

Dried lavender

Contrasting embroidery floss (optional)

Hot-glue gun (optional)

Appliqués, crochet trims, vintage buttons, and/or other trimmings

One 13in (33cm) length of thong, ribbon, string, or strong thread per tag

2 For fabric, stitch a ¼in (5mm) seam around the edges, pivoting the fabric at the corners and leaving an opening at one side, then snip off the seam allowances at the corners, turn the tag right side out, and use a blunt-ended tool to push out the corners. For felt, simply use tiny running stitches to hand sew a narrow seam around the edges, leaving a small opening.

3 Following the manufacturer's instructions, attach a grommet (eyelet) ¼in (5mm) down from the top, centered between the side edges.

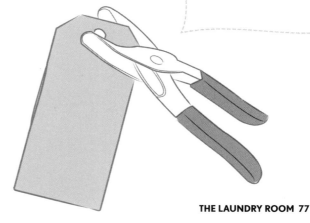

4 Insert a small amount of dried lavender into the tag through the opening. For fabric, turn in the seam allowances of the opening and slipstitch it closed. For felt, hand sew the remainder of the seam closed, using running stitch.

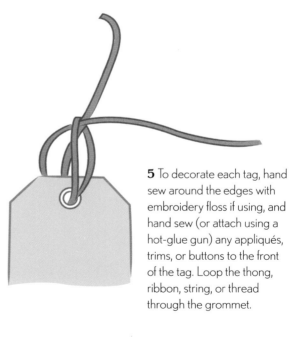

5 To decorate each tag, hand sew around the edges with embroidery floss if using, and hand sew (or attach using a hot-glue gun) any appliqués, trims, or buttons to the front of the tag. Loop the thong, ribbon, string, or thread through the grommet.

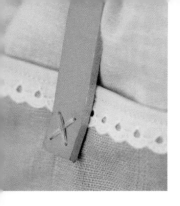

bag storage

This linen grocery-bag dispenser is a stylish take on a drawstring bag dispenser, keeping bags neatly stored out of sight. It features a strong leather bridle handle strap at the top so you can hang it up, pretty eyelet (broderie anglaise) trim, and a pop of contrasting color in the binding and top panel.

you will need

Pearlized acrylic paint and small paintbrush

One 16⅛in (41cm) length of (¾in-) (20mm-) wide bridle leather

One 4 x 20in (10 x 50cm) rectangle of lining fabric or coordinating fabric for upper panel

Matching sewing thread

One 17 x 20in (44 x 50cm) rectangle of linen fabric for lower panel

One 14¼ x 20in (36 x 50cm) rectangle of heavyweight fusible interfacing

One 20in (50cm) length of eyelet (broderie anglaise) trim

One 20in (50cm) length of ½in- (15mm-) wide bias tape (bias binding) in a coordinating color

Two 4in (10cm) lengths of elastic cord

Embroidery floss to match upper panel

1 With a small paintbrush, carefully paint the edges of the leather strip and leave to dry.

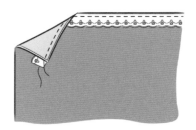

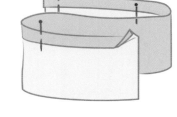

2 To make the top casing, turn under and press ¼in (5mm) and then ¾in (1.5cm) along the long top edge of the rectangle for the upper panel. Stitch in place close to the turned-under edge. Make a casing along the bottom edge of the lower (linen) panel in the same way.

3 Following the manufacturer's instructions, iron the interfacing to the wrong side of the lower panel, with one long edge of the interfacing even with the long top edge of the lower panel. Now pin the eyelet (broderie anglaise) trim around the top edge of the lower panel, on the right side, with raw edges even. Machine baste in place.

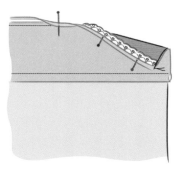

4 Pin the top edge of the lower panel to the bottom edge of the upper panel, with wrong sides together and raw edges even. Machine baste together and then bind the raw edges together, as shown on page 12. Press the upper panel away from the lower panel.

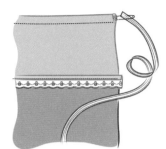

5 Attach a safety pin to one of the lengths of elastic, and thread the safety pin through the casing on the upper panel, pulling the elastic through with it. Stitch the ends of the elastic in place ³⁄₈in (1cm) from the ends of the casing. Repeat for the other length of elastic and the casing at the bottom of the lower panel.

6 To attach the handle, use a water-soluble marker or a dressmaker's pencil to mark the positions for four holes on each end of the leather strap. Make the holes using a craft pick (see page 14). Using embroidery floss, and sewing through the marks to form an X-shape at each end, attach the ends of the strap 1¼in (3cm) down from the bound edge of the lower panel and 5in (12cm) from the raw side edges of the panel. Be careful not to catch in the upper panel.

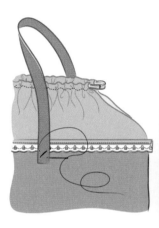

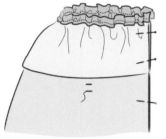

7 Fold the bag dispenser in half lengthwise, with right sides together and raw edges even. Pin the side edges securely together and stitch a ³⁄₈in (1cm) seam from top to bottom. Zigzag the raw edges of the seam allowance separately, and press the seam open. Turn the bag dispenser right side out, and fill with plastic bags.

storage cube

Storage cubes have a multitude of uses—in the laundry room to store clean cloths, in the kitchen to hold cloth napkins, or in the hallway to contain gloves, scarves, or mail. Use different prints on each side, mix and match the binding colors, or pretty them up with crochet trims. Make the cubes in various sizes simply by adjusting the size of the squares.

1 Following the manufacturer's instructions, iron interfacing to the wrong side of each of the five print-fabric squares. Lay out four of the squares on your work surface, right side up, with the prints facing the same direction. Pin two adjacent squares together at the side edges, with right sides together and raw edges even; stitch a ³/₈in (1cm) seam, starting at the top edge and finishing ³/₈in (1cm) from the bottom edge. Repeat to join the other side edges, forming the sides of your cube. Press the seams open.

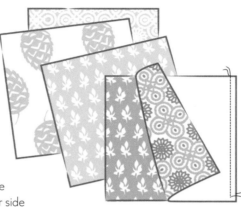

you will need

Five 7in (18cm) squares each of printed fabric and heavyweight fusible interfacing, per cube

Five 6³/₄in (17.5cm) squares of fabric for lining, per cube

Matching sewing thread

One 25½in (69cm) length of ³/₄in- (20mm-) wide crochet or eyelet (broderie anglaise) trim (optional), per cube

One 25½in (69cm) length of ½in- (15mm-) wide bias tape (bias binding), per cube

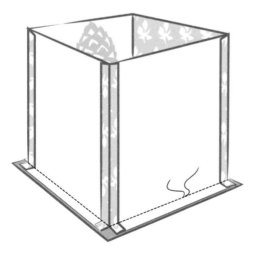

2 Pin the remaining print-fabric square to the bottom edges of the other four, with right sides together, raw edges even, and corners matching. Stitch a ³/₈in (1cm) seam around all four edges, pivoting the fabric at the corners. (The unstitched portions at the ends of the side seams will open up to allow you to do this.) Press the seam open.

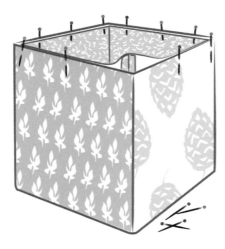

3 Repeat steps 1 and 2 for the lining, omitting the interfacing. With the print-fabric cube right side out and the lining cube wrong side out, place the lining inside the print-fabric cube, so they are wrong sides together. Check that the seams are lined up, then pin in place. Machine baste the lining and print fabric together around all four sides, ¼in (5mm) from the top edge.

4 If desired, pin crochet or eyelet (broderie anglaise) trim around the outside, with the top edge of the trim slightly less than ³⁄₈in (1cm) from the top edge of the cube, turning under the ends by ¼in (5mm) each and butting them together; machine baste in place. Use the bias tape (bias binding) to bind the top edges of the cube, as shown on page 12, covering the raw edge of the trim if used.

ironing board cover

Make ironing less of a tedious chore by replacing your old ironing board cover with a cheerful new made-to-measure cover in pretty fabric. Lining the cover with cotton batting (wadding) gives a lovely padded base, while the elastic cord will allow you to quickly and easily remove and refit the cover whenever it needs laundering.

you will need

One rectangle each of cotton canvas fabric and cotton batting (wadding), 2¾in (7cm) wider and longer than your ironing board

One length of ½in- (15mm-) wide bias tape (bias binding), long enough to go around your entire ironing board cover, plus ¾in (2cm)

Elastic cord, long enough to go around your entire ironing board

Two beads to thread onto ends of elastic cord (optional)

1 Using a water-soluble marker or a dressmaker's pencil, transfer the shape of your ironing board onto the wrong side of the cotton canvas, adding 1³⁄₈in (3.5cm) all the way around. Cut out the shape. Use this piece as a pattern to draw around on the cotton batting (wadding). With the edges even, pin the batting to the wrong side of the canvas. Baste (tack) together around the edges.

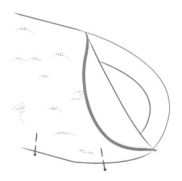

2 Turn ³⁄₈in (1cm) to the wrong side on one end of the bias tape (bias binding). Starting at the square end of the cover, pin the bias tape around the entire cover, with right sides together and the fold line ³⁄₈in (1cm) from the edge. Ease the tape around the curved corners, but be careful not to stretch it. When you get back to your starting point, cut off the excess tape, leaving ³⁄₈in (1cm) extra. Turn ³⁄₈in (1cm) to the wrong side at this end, and pin in place so the two folded ends of the tape butt together. Stitch the tape in place ³⁄₈in (1cm) from the edge of the fabric, but do not stitch over the join between the two tape ends as you will insert the elastic cord through this gap. Finish binding the edge (see page 12).

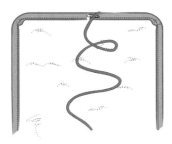

3 Attach a small safety pin to one end of the elastic cord. Thread the safety pin and cord through the opening in the bias tape, through the casing, and back out through the opening.

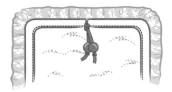

4 Place the cover over the ironing board and pull up the elastic so that the cover folds underneath and fits tightly. Tie the ends of the elastic in a double bow and trim off any excess. Or, if you prefer, thread a decorative bead onto each end of the cord, knotting the cord ends to hold them in place.

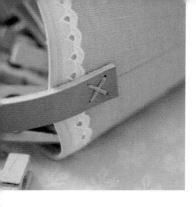

linen basket

This super-stylish linen basket has a number of storage uses, from laundry or towels to bed linen or toys. Linen gives it a rustic feel and looks great combined with eyelet (broderie anglaise) trim. For the interior fabric I chose a textured cotton lining in a duck-egg blue and painted the leather handles to match.

you will need

Pearlized acrylic paint and small paintbrush

Two 13in (33.5cm) lengths of ¾in- (20mm-) wide bridle leather

One 14¾ x 10¼in (37.5 x 26cm) rectangle each of linen, lining fabric, and stiff interfacing, for base

Two 14¾ x 10¼in (37.5 x 26cm) rectangles of heavyweight fusible interfacing, for base

One 43¼ x 11in (110 x 28cm) rectangle each of linen and lining fabric, for sides

Two 43¼ x 11in (110 x 28cm) rectangles of heavyweight fusible interfacing for sides

Matching sewing thread

1¼yd (1.1m) of eyelet (broderie anglaise) trim with one finished edge

1¼yd (1.1m) of ½in- (15mm-) wide bias tape (bias binding)

Embroidery floss (thread) to match lining

dimensions

The finished linen basket measures 14in (35.5cm) wide x 9½in (24cm) deep x 10½in (27cm) high, excluding handles.

1 With a small paintbrush, carefully paint the edges of the leather strips with pearlized paint, and leave to dry.

2 Using a water-soluble marker or a dressmaker's pencil, transfer the base template on page 137 to the wrong side of the linen, lining fabric, stiff interfacing, and heavyweight interfacing, and cut out the shapes—you need two of the heavyweight interfacing and one each of the other three. Following the manufacturer's instructions, iron the heavyweight interfacing to the wrong side of the linen base and the lining base. Also iron heavyweight fusible interfacing to the wrong side of the linen and lining side pieces.

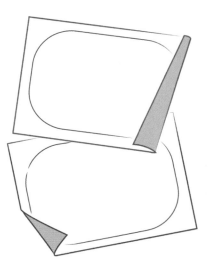

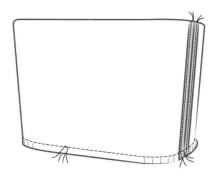

3 Pin the two shorter edges of the linen side piece with right sides together and raw edges even. Stitch a ⅜in (1cm) seam, stopping ⅜in (1cm) from the lower edge; press the seam open. Topstitch ¼in (7mm) from each side of the seam line. Staystitch (see page 9) slightly less than ⅜in (1cm) from the lower edge, and snip into the curved seam allowance at regular intervals.

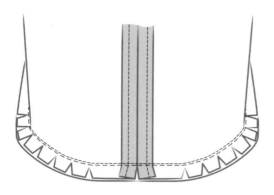

4 With right sides together and raw edges even, pin the lower edge of the linen side piece all around the edge of the linen base, lining up the seam so that it is in the center of one of the ends. The snips in the seam allowance on the lower edge will open up to allow it to fit onto the base. Stitch a ³⁄₈in (1cm) seam all around.

5 Repeat steps 3 and 4 for the lining pieces, omitting the topstitching of the seam. Lay the stiff interfacing for the base (which you cut out in step 2) on the base, and hand sew it to the seam allowance in a few places. With the linen right side out and the lining wrong side out, slip the lining inside the linen so that the two layers have their wrong sides together and the seams are lined up. Pin and then machine baste ¼in (5mm) from the top edge.

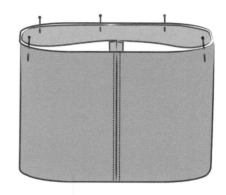

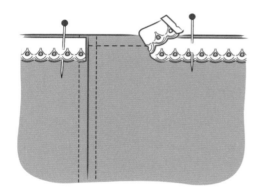

6 Starting at the seam, pin eyelet (broderie anglaise) trim to the right side of the linen all around the top edge, aligning the straight edge of the trim with the raw edge of the linen. When you get back to your starting point, turn under ¼in (5mm) on the end, and lap this over the raw edge of the starting end. Machine baste ¼in (5mm) from the top edge.

7 Use the bias tape (bias binding) to bind the top edge, as shown on page 12. Mark four holes at each end of the two straps, and attach the handles to opposite sides of the basket with embroidery floss (see page 14). The ends of each strap should be 2¼in (6cm) from the top, and 2¾in (7cm) apart.

variation: clothespin basket

Perfect for holding clothespins, this little linen basket can always be hung up in the hallway to store knickknacks or in the living room to hold the remote controls. It is made in much the same way as the laundry basket, but using the two templates on page 140 to cut one base and two side pieces, which are seamed together. Rather than two handles, it has just one, made from a 12in (31cm) length of 5/8in- (16mm-) wide bridle leather, attached 1 3/8in (3.5cm) from the top.

Chapter 6

The Bedroom

It's not always possible to find exactly the elements your bedroom needs, but sewing them yourself can solve the problem, allowing you to create exactly what you want. I designed these projects for my new guest bedroom, combining contemporary colors with vintage patterned fabrics and on-trend linen. There's a padded headboard that is a great way to update your bed, and fun pompom-trimmed throw pillows to accompany it. Add decor with colorful felt-flower garland lights and a ruffled bed throw. Keep your bedroom clutter-free with an assortment of coordinating bags that will hold everything from makeup to clothing. Finally, to make sure you get a good night's sleep, there is a beautiful eye mask—and even this coordinates with the decor.

padded headboard

Made from linen and decorated with covered buttons, used for the button-tufting, this simple headboard rests on the bedstead or mattress, while the ties at the top, looped over hooks on the wall, prevent it from tipping forward. And not only is it very pretty, but it is supremely comfortable to lean against when reading in bed.

1 Pin a length of lace, ribbon, or twill tape to the right side of the upper gusset strip, ³⁄₈in (1cm) from one end, and equidistant from the long edges. Repeat at the other end of the upper gusset strip, and then space the remaining three lengths evenly between them. Stitch in place as shown. Be careful not to catch the ends of these ties in the seams you stitch in steps 2–4.

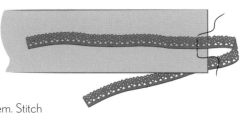

2 To assemble the gusset, pin each end of the upper gusset strip to one end of each side gusset strip with right sides together. Pin each end of the lower gusset strip to the other end of each side gusset strip. Stitch ³⁄₈in (1cm) seams, starting and stopping ³⁄₈in (1cm) from the ends of each seam. Press the seams open.

3 Pin the front panel to the front edge of the gusset, with right sides together and raw edges even, matching the seams in the gusset with the corners of the front panel. Stitch a ³⁄₈in (1cm) seam around all four edges, pivoting the fabric at the corners. (The unstitched portions at the ends of the gusset seams will open up to allow you to do this.)

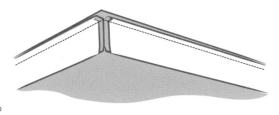

you will need

Five 16in (40cm) lengths of lace, ribbon, or twill tape, for ties

Two 2¾ x 60in (7 x 152cm) strips of linen, for upper and lower gussets

Two 2¾ x 20½in (7 x 52cm) strips of linen, for side gussets

Two 20½ x 60in (52 x 152cm) rectangles of linen, for front and back panels

Matching sewing thread

100 percent polyester high-loft fiberfill toy filling

Matte embroidery cotton or embroidery floss (thread)

Embroidery needle and upholstery needle

Thirty-two ⁵⁄₈in (15mm) covered buttons (see page 14)

Five hooks with appropriate fittings

dimensions

The finished headboard measures 19 x 55 x 2in (48 x 140 x 5cm) and fits a standard double bed. (To make it in a different size, see Tip on page 96.)

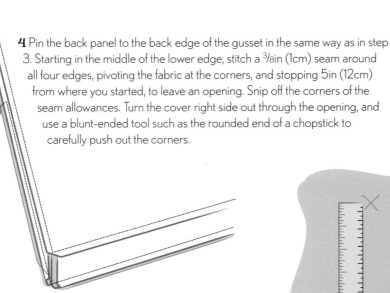

4 Pin the back panel to the back edge of the gusset in the same way as in step 3. Starting in the middle of the lower edge, stitch a ³⁄₈in (1cm) seam around all four edges, pivoting the fabric at the corners, and stopping 5in (12cm) from where you started, to leave an opening. Snip off the corners of the seam allowances. Turn the cover right side out through the opening, and use a blunt-ended tool such as the rounded end of a chopstick to carefully push out the corners.

TIP DIFFERENT SIZED-HEADBOARD To fit a different-sized bed, measure the width and add 5in (12cm). Similarly, you could make the headboard a different height—just add 1½in (4cm) to the desired finished height. You may need to alter the number of buttons and ties to correspond.

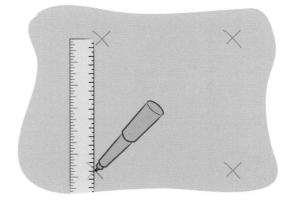

5 Using a water-soluble pen or a dressmaker's pencil, mark where your buttons will go on the right side of the front and in the corresponding places on the right side of the back. Here, the 16 pairs of buttons are spaced 6in (15cm) apart. Stuff the cover with filling, as explained in step 4 of the Garden Kneeler, page 129. Turn in the seam allowances of the opening and slipstitch closed.

6 With an embroidery needle threaded with embroidery cotton, hand sew running stitch ³⁄₈in (1cm) from the edge around the entire headboard on both the front and back panels. The stitching should go through both the front/back panel and the gusset, creating a narrow flange all around the front and another around the back.

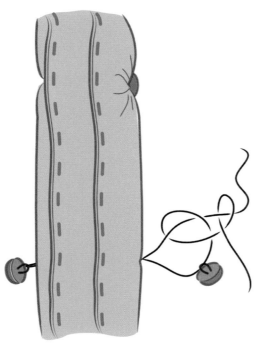

7 For the button-tufting, thread a long upholstery needle with embroidery cotton. Starting with one of the central pairs of marks done in step 5, insert the needle into the mark at the back. While holding on to the end of the embroidery cotton, push the needle through the padding and the mark on the front, then through the shank of a button, then back through the front mark and padding, and out again at the back where it first went in. Now thread it through the shank of a second button and tie the ends in a slip knot, as shown. Pull the ends tight and fasten securely. Repeat for the remaining buttons. Mount the hooks on the wall so that one will be above each tie and at a height to allow the headboard to sit on the bed. Fasten the ties and loop them over the hooks.

laundry bag

This ultra-feminine ruffled laundry bag is the perfect holder for those lacy pieces that have to be washed on the "delicate" setting. When not in use, it still makes a delightful addition to your room decor. You could also use it to keep all your delicates together in your suitcase when you are traveling, or to hold your favorite shoes or clutch bags.

you will need

Ten 15in (38cm) lengths of 1in- (25mm-) wide eyelet (broderie anglaise) trim with one finished edge

Matching sewing thread

One 12¾ x 43½in (32 x 110cm) rectangle of linen

Two 33in (84cm) lengths of ⅜in- (10mm-) wide grosgrain ribbon

dimensions

The finished laundry bag measures 12 x 19in (30 x 48cm).

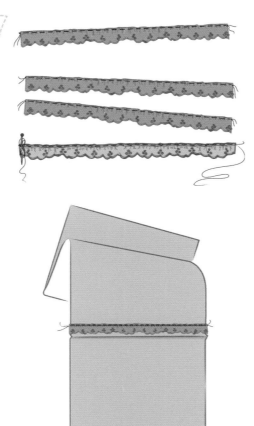

1 Machine baste along the long raw edge of the trim, leaving long threads at each end. At one end, secure the bobbin thread by wrapping it in a figure-eight around a pin. Gently pull on the other end of the bobbin thread to gather the trim, sliding the gathers along the thread until the whole piece is slightly gathered and is 12½in (32cm) long. Knot the threads at both ends. Repeat to make eight more ruffles. On the remaining length of trim, turn ¼in (5mm) to the wrong side along the long raw edge, and press. Machine baste along the pressed edge through both layers, and then gather up the trim as above. Set it aside to use at the end of the next step.

2 Fold the linen rectangle in half crosswise, with right sides together, and press the crease (which will eventually be at the bottom of the bag). Unfold it again. Pin the first ruffle in place on the right side, with the bottom edge of the ruffle lining up with the crease. Topstitch in place close to the raw edge. Pin the next ruffle above it, with its bottom edge overlapping the raw edge on the previous ruffle. Topstitch. Continue in this way, finishing with the hemmed ruffle you had set aside.

3 Fold the linen in half again along the crease line, with right sides together, enclosing the ruffles. Pin the side edges together. Starting from the bottom, stitch a ³/₈in (1cm) seam up one side edge, stopping 5in (13cm) from the top. Start stitching again ¾in (2cm) further along the seam line, and continue to the top. Repeat for the other side edge. Press open the seams. Zigzag the raw edges separately. Zigzag the raw edge all around the top of the bag. Turn the bag the right way out and press (re-pressing the bottom crease now that it is right side out).

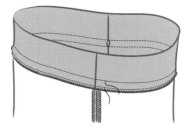

4 To create the drawstring channel, turn 2¾in (7cm) to the wrong side at the top of the bag. Press and pin in place. Stitch ³/₈in (1cm) above this edge all around the bag. Stitch another row of stitching ¾in (2cm) above the first line of stitching to create a channel that is in line with the openings in the side seams on the right side. Use a safety pin to thread one drawstring ribbon through the entire channel until it comes out at the starting point. Repeat with second ribbon, but from the opposite opening. Knot the ends together at each side and pull the ribbons to close.

variation: ruffled bed throw

Overlapping rows of eyelet (broderie anglaise) ruffles also look great on this throw. You will need to cut the lengths of eyelet to the width of your throw plus 20 percent. Cut out front and back panels from linen, and a piece of batting (wadding) the same size. Baste (tack) the batting to the back panel, and decorate the front with rows of ruffles as in steps 1 and 2. Now join the front and back together as for steps 6 and 7 of the Pieced Throw, page 64.

pompom pillow

Pompoms look great as a trim on pillows covered in vintage fabrics. Finding the right vintage textile takes time and effort, so I like to use it just for the front of a pillow, with a contrasting fabric for the back. Make a pair of these fun pillows to adorn your bed.

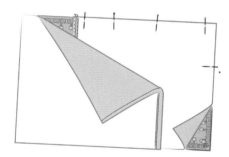

you will need

One 61in (154cm) length of pompom trim

One 18¾ x 12¾in (48 x 32cm) rectangle of vintage fabric for the front

Two 15 x 13¼in (38 x 32cm) rectangles of linen for the back

Matching sewing thread

One 19in (48cm) length of narrow rickrack

18 x 12in (46 x 30cm) pillow form (cushion pad)

dimensions

The finished pillow measures 18 x 12in (46cm x 30cm).

1 Pin the pompom trim to the right side of the vintage fabric just under ⅜in (1cm) in from every edge, with the pompoms facing toward the center. Try to get a pompom at each corner, though it may not always be possible. Stitch the trim in place ⅜in (1cm) from the edge.

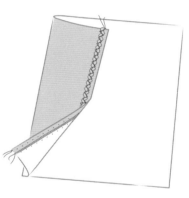

2 On one short edge of one back piece, press and pin a double ⅜in (1cm) hem, as shown in step 1 of Crochet-trimmed Napkin on page 48. Stitch in place ⅛in (3mm) from the inner fold. Repeat for the other back piece. On the right side of one back piece, pin rickrack over the stitching; zigzag in place.

3 Pin the back piece that has the rickrack to the front piece, with right sides together and raw edges even. Place the other back piece, wrong side up, on top of the first back piece, matching the raw edges with those of the front. The hemmed edges of the two back pieces will overlap by about 9½in (24cm).

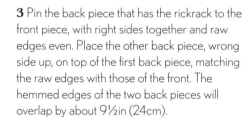

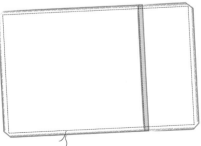

4 Stitch a ⅜in (1cm) seam around all four edges, pivoting the fabric at the corners. Snip off the corners of the seam allowances and zigzag the raw edges. Turn the cover right side out and use a blunt-ended tool, such as the rounded end of a chopstick, to carefully push out the corners. Press the cover and insert the pillow form (cushion pad).

round buttoned pillow

This classic throw pillow looks great in any living room, regardless of the decor, and its different elements—front, back, gusset, piping, covered buttons—give you plenty of scope for incorporating contrasting fabrics. The same pillow in a soft green colorway can be seen in the center of the sofa on page 54.

you will need

One 43 x 3½in (109 x 9cm) rectangle each of fabric and fusible interfacing, for gusset

Two 43in (109cm) lengths each of bias tape (bias binding) and piping cord

Matching sewing thread

Two 43 x 8in (109 x 20cm) rectangles of fabric, for top and bottom

100 percent high-loft polyester toy filling

Embroidery floss (thread) in same color as fabric

Embroidery needle and upholstery needle

Two 1in (25mm) covered buttons (see page 14)

dimensions

The finished pillow measures 13¼in (34cm) in diameter and is 2¾in (7cm) deep.

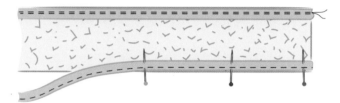

1 Following the manufacturer's instructions, iron the interfacing to the fabric piece for the gusset. Using the bias tape (bias binding) and piping cord, make two 43in (109cm) lengths of piping, as shown on page 12. Pin one length of the piping along the upper edge of the interfaced gusset strip, with right sides together and raw edges even. The piping cord itself should be ⅜in (1cm) from the edge. Using a zipper foot, machine baste in place as close to the piping cord as possible. Repeat to attach the other length of piping to the lower edge of the gusset.

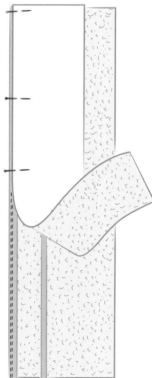

2 With right sides together, pin one long edge of one large fabric rectangle to one long edge of the gusset, with right sides together and raw edges even, sandwiching the piping between the two pieces. Using a zipper foot, stitch a ⅜in (1cm) seam, as close as possible to the piping cord. Repeat to attach the remaining large fabric rectangle to the other long edge of the gusset.

3 Fold the entire piece in half crosswise, with right sides together, aligning the raw edges and the ends of the piping. Pin the two ends of the piece together, forming a cylinder, then stitch a ³⁄₈in (1cm) seam. Press the seam open.

4 Press ³⁄₈in (1cm) to the wrong side along the top and bottom raw edges of this cylinder. Thread an embroidery needle with floss (thread). Starting at the seam, hand sew running stitch along each pressed-under edge. On the lower edge, pull up the ends of this floss to gather up the bottom of the pillow as tight as it will go, around the center of the bottom panel. Tie a tight knot and trim off the excess floss.

5 Grab a generous handful of filling and gently pull it loose, repeating the process two or three times. With the pillow right side out and sitting on its gathered end, insert the filling through the opening, pushing it out to the edges. Continue until you have a firm, plump pillow. Now gather up the opening, tie a knot, and trim off the excess, as you did in step 4.

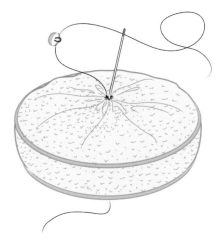

6 Use an upholstery needle threaded with embroidery floss to attach a covered button to the center of the pillow front, and another to the center of the back, using the button-tufting technique explained in step 7 of the Padded Headboard, page 97.

eye mask

This pretty eye mask with its lace elastic strap helps to ensure a perfect night's restful and relaxing sleep. Eye masks also make a really special, stylish, and thoughtful gift.

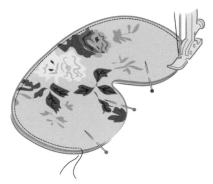

you will need

One 9 x 4¼in (23 x 11cm) rectangle each of print cotton fabric, cotton lining fabric, and cotton batting (wadding)

Matching sewing thread

One 24in (60cm) length of ½in-(15mm-) wide bias tape (bias binding)

One 12in (31cm) length of decorative elastic

1 Transfer the template on page 138 onto the wrong side of your fabric, using a water-soluble marker or a dressmaker's pencil; you will need one piece. Cut out the piece. Repeat for the lining fabric and the batting (wadding).

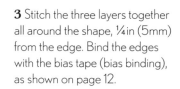

2 Sandwich the batting piece between the print fabric and lining fabric pieces, with the right side of each fabric piece facing outward. Pin around the edges.

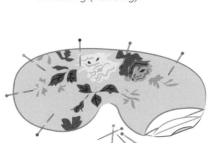

3 Stitch the three layers together all around the shape, ¼in (5mm) from the edge. Bind the edges with the bias tape (bias binding), as shown on page 12.

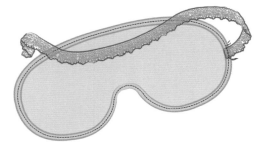

4 At the back of the eye mask, turn under ¼in (5mm) on one end of the elastic and pin it to the binding at one side; stitch in place on top of the existing stitching. Check the length of the elastic for fit, and trim off the excess elastic, leaving an extra ¼in (5mm) to turn under. Attach this end to the other side of the eye mask, in the same way as for the first end.

makeup bag

Made from a beautiful vintage fabric (one of my favorite fabrics—you can see it used in several projects in this book!), stabilized with interfacing, and lined with a contrast fabric, this makeup bag is a great way to create a bag that stands up all by itself. You can easily adjust the measurements to make it larger or smaller to suit your needs. I love to leave one filled with hotel-sized bottles of toiletries in my guest bedroom, which comes in handy for visitors who may have forgotten something.

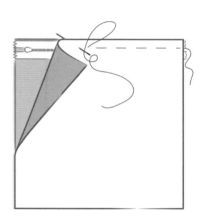

1 Following the manufacturer's instructions, iron the interfacing to the wrong side of both print fabric pieces. Place the closed zipper, face down, along the top edge of the right side of one interfaced fabric piece, with raw edges even and with the zipper pull at the left, ⅜in (1cm) in from the side edge. Now place a lining piece right side down on top, lining up its raw edges with the edges of the interfaced fabric piece. Pin in place through all the layers. Hand baste (tack), then remove the pins. With the zipper foot on the machine, stitch just above the zipper teeth.

you will need

Two rectangles each of print fabric, cotton fabric for the lining, and medium-weight fusible interfacing, 8¾in (22cm) wide by 9in (23cm) high

Matching sewing thread

8in (20cm) nylon zipper

One 6¼in (16cm) length of narrow rickrack for zipper pull

dimensions

The finished make-up bag measures 6¼in (16cm) high, 3½in (9cm) thick, and 8in (20cm) wide at the top

2 Pull the pieces of fabric away from the seam, so they are wrong sides together and the zipper is exposed. Lay the raw edge of the closed zipper face down along the top edge of the right side of the other interfaced piece, with raw edges even, with the zipper pull at the right this time, ⅜in (1cm) from the side edge. Place the other lining piece on top, as in step 1. Pin and then hand baste in place, and stitch just above the zipper teeth, with the zipper foot on the machine. Take care not to catch in any of the fabric that you attached in step 1.

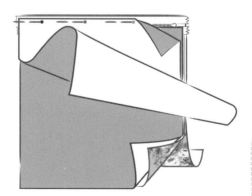

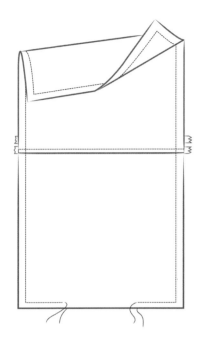

3 Reposition the fabric pieces so that the two print pieces are facing right sides together and the two lining pieces are also facing right sides together, with the zipper in between. Line up the raw edges, pin them together at either end of the zipper, and then open the zipper, before pinning all around the edges. Stitch a ³⁄₈in (1cm) seam around the edges, pivoting the fabric at the corners and leaving an opening at what will be the bottom edge of the lining.

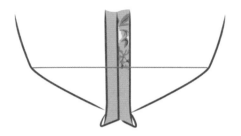

4 At one corner of the print fabric pieces, separate the two fabric layers and rearrange them so that the bottom seam and the side seam are aligned down the center, and the pouch body comes away from the corner in a triangular shape. Press the seams open. Using a ruler and a water-soluble pen, mark the line at right angles to the seam 1¼in (3cm) from the tip of the corner.

5 Stitch along the line, then snip off the corner, leaving a ¼in (5mm) seam allowance. Repeat steps 4 and 5—known as boxing the corners—for the other printed-fabric corner and for both lining corners.

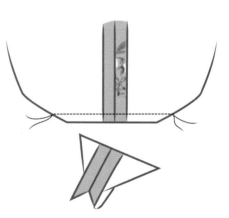

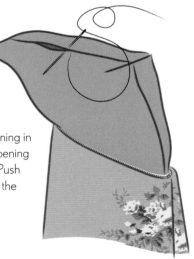

6 Turn the pouch right side out through the opening in the lining. Fold in the seam allowances on the opening and slipstitch the edges together (see page 11). Push the lining into the bag. Tie a length of rickrack to the zipper pull, knotting the ends.

variation: leather-handled bag

I use this bag to dress up my guest bedroom and store my latest magazines for guests to read. Made from a vintage floral fabric that has been stabilized with interfacing, the bag has leather handles and a useful inner pocket. It is made in the same way as the Two-Print Bag on page 18, except that the front and back are cut in just one piece. This is because it doesn't have separate panels of contrast fabrics, and because the fabric is a two-way print, meaning that the pattern works upside down, too. You need one 14¾ x 34½in (37 x 88cm) rectangle each of the outer fabric and the medium-weight fusible interfacing, plus a 14¾ x 32¼in (37 x 82cm) rectangle of lining fabric. The other materials, including the pieces for the pocket, are the same as for the Two-Print Bag. Make the bag as for steps 1–3 and 6–9.

rose garland

Easy to sew, this rose garland makes a colorful decoration strung above a bed, looped over hooks on the wall, or used as a party decoration. As it incorporates battery-powered lights, you could also use it as atmospheric lighting outdoors in dry weather, though it wouldn't be rainproof.

One 8¼ x 12in (21 x 30cm) rectangle of felt for each rose

Battery-powered Christmas tree mini-lights

Hot-glue gun

1 For each rose, cut out the pieces from the felt rectangle as for the Rose Brooch on page 28, step 1, using the templates on page 139. In the center of one of the five large felt pieces, use small, sharp scissors to make a small hole.

2 Feed a light bulb through the hole in the felt piece, with the wires coming out of the back. Using a hot-glue gun, secure the bulb in place on the felt.

3 Complete the rose as for the Rose Brooch on pages 28-29, steps 2-5, using the hot-glue gun to secure each piece rather than hand sewing them in place.

4 Repeat the above steps until you have a felt rose on each bulb.

Chapter 7

In The Garden

I love gardening and entertaining alfresco. Now that outdoor spaces have become extensions of our homes, I have put together a selection of sewing projects that enable you to take your home-decorating style outside. You can turn a simple bench into a comfy sofa with a stylish cushion, enhanced by the bolster and pillows from the living room chapter. And why not update your deckchairs with new slings? Learn how to create a charming wigwam for the perfect shady spot on a summer's day and adorn it with bunting made from crocheted doilies. There are projects for stylish gardening, with a garden kneeler and a gardener's apron. If you are like me, your designer's eye won't fail to notice how much they brighten up your shed walls where they hang!

bench cushion

The cover for this bench cushion is easy to make and also easy to remove for laundering, thanks to the zipper at the back. I chose two different prints, one for the top and bottom, and one for the gusset. The cushion is ideal for an outdoor bench and also for a window seat.

you will need

Foam precut to desired finished size of cushion

Two rectangles of cotton canvas, each 39in (100cm) long by half the height of the foam plus ¾in (2cm), for the gusset zipper panel

One 39in (100cm) zipper to match fabric

Two rectangles of cotton canvas, each half the length of the foam minus 18³⁄₈in (47cm) by the height of the foam plus ¾in (2cm), for the gusset back

Two rectangles of cotton canvas, each the width of the foam plus ¾in (2cm) by the height of the foam plus ¾in (2cm), for the gusset ends

One rectangle of cotton canvas, the length of the foam plus ¾in (2cm) by the height of the foam plus ¾in (2cm), for the gusset front

Two rectangles of cotton canvas, each the width (front-to-back) of the foam plus ¾in (2cm) by the length (side-to-side) of the foam plus ¾in (2cm), for the top and bottom

Matching sewing thread

dimensions

The finished cushion pictured here measures 18 x 44 x 2in (46 x 112 x 5cm), but you can adjust the measurements to suit your seating (see You Will Need).

1 Pin the two gusset zipper panel pieces with right sides together, and machine baste a ¾in (2cm) seam down one long edge. Apply the zipper to the seam (see page 13) and remove the basting. With right sides together, pin one short edge of one of the gusset back pieces to one end of the zipper panel. Stitch a ³⁄₈in (1cm) seam. Repeat to attach the other gusset back piece to the other end of the zipper panel.

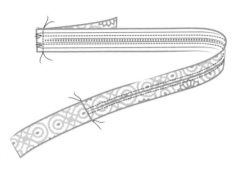

TIP USING FOAM Foam comes in various qualities and thicknesses; the foam used here is 2in (5cm) thick. Because it is very difficult to cut, getting the supplier to cut it to size is recommended.

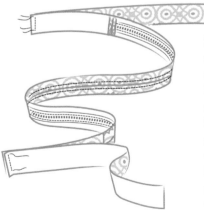

2 With right sides together, pin one short edge of a gusset end piece to one short edge of the gusset back. Stitch a ³⁄₈in (1cm) seam, starting and stopping ³⁄₈in (1cm) from the ends of the seam. Repeat to attach the other gusset end piece to the other short edge of the gusset back. Finally, join the remaining short edge of each gusset end piece to the short edges of the gusset front in the same way. Press the seams open.

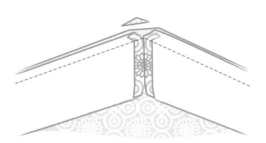

3 Pin the upper edge of the gusset to the top piece, with right sides together and matching the corner seams to the corners of the top piece. Stitch a ³⁄₈in (1cm) seam around all four edges, pivoting the fabric at the corners. (The unstitched portions at the ends of the gusset seams will open up to allow you to do this.) Snip off the seam allowances at the corners.

4 Open the zipper, pin the lower edge of the gusset to the bottom piece, and stitch together as in step 3. Turn the cover right side out and use a blunt-ended tool, such as the rounded end of a chopstick, to carefully push out the corners. Press the cover, insert the foam, and close the zipper.

deckchair sling

If, like me, you have an old deckchair that has seen better days, why not replace the sling with a pretty, new one to give it a fresh lease on life? This deckchair sling has slots at either end to slide wooden dowels through, and it should fit most regular collapsible wooden frames. If in doubt, measure your old sling and adjust as necessary.

you will need

One 18½ x 49½in (47 x 126cm) piece of cotton canvas fabric

Two 18½in (47cm) lengths of ½in- (15mm-) wide bias tape (bias binding)

Matching sewing thread

Two 49½in (126cm) lengths of 1in- (25mm-) wide eyelet (broderie anglaise) trim

Two 49½in (126cm) lengths of narrow rickrack

dimensions

The finished deckchair sling is 17¼in (44cm) wide, excluding trim, and 45in (114cm) long.

1 Bind the two shorter edges of the canvas rectangle, as shown on page 12. Turn ⅝in (1.5cm) to the wrong side on each of the two long edges, and press.

2 Pin a length of eyelet (broderie anglais) trim under each pressed edge so that the decorative edge projects beyond the hemmed edge. Stitch ⅜in (1cm) from the edge. For extra strength, stitch again ¼in (5mm) from the edge.

3 On the right side, pin rickrack over the double row of stitching, and either stitch in place or hand sew it in place using a decorative stitch.

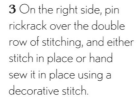

4 Turn under 2¼in (6cm) on each of the bound edges; press. Pin in place. Stitch as close to each bound edge as you can, and then stitch again ⅜in (1cm) from each edge, creating a double row of stitching.

wigwam

Create a little hideaway in your backyard, a shady spot for sunny days. Children will love holding tea parties with their friends and favorite toys in this pretty wigwam, and it also provides a great place for adults to read or take a quiet afternoon nap! Decorate it with crochet doily bunting (see page 134), a comfy patchwork mat (see page 126), and a selection of soft pillows and cushions.

1 Following the cutting layout on page 142, draw the shapes on the wrong side of the fabric, using a long straightedge and a water-soluble marker or a dressmaker's pencil. Start with one door piece, which is 9¾in (24.5cm) wide on the selvage and 17¾in (45cm) wide on the scalloped edge. Draw six triangles with their bases on the selvage and their pointed tops on the scalloped edge—the bases should be 16in (41cm) wide, and the triangles 16in (41cm) apart. These will be the top pieces. The fabric between the triangles will be the five bottom pieces and should each be 32in (82cm) wide on the scalloped edge. At the far end of the fabric, draw a second door, the mirror image of the first. Cut out all the pieces, then cut off the upper point on each of the six top pieces so that the upper edge of each is 2¼in (6cm) wide.

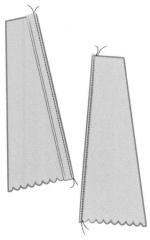

2 To stop the lengths of ribbon from fraying, paint the ends with fray-stop liquid and leave to dry. Using the bias tape (bias binding), bind the two edges (see page 12) that were at the ends of the fabric, which will be the inner edges of the two doors.

you will need

5½yd (5m) of 44in- (112cm-) or 45in- (115cm-) wide fabric

Two 26in (66cm) lengths of ³⁄₈in- (10mm-) wide ribbon

Twenty-four 12in (30cm) lengths of ³⁄₈in- (10mm-) wide ribbon

Fray-stop liquid

Bias tape (bias binding)

Matching sewing thread

Six wooden poles, each 8ft (2.4m) long and ¾in (21mm) thick

Electric drill and vise

Strong string or jute

dimensions

The finished wigwam is 62½in (160cm) across and about 86in (218cm) high.

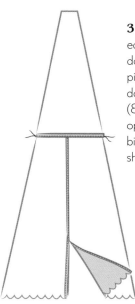

3 With right sides together and raw edges even, pin the upper edge of each door to the lower edge of the same top piece, with the bound edges of the doors overlapping each other by 3½in (8cm). Stitch a ³⁄₈in (1cm) seam, press open the seam to give a neat finish, then bind the seam allowances together as shown on page 12.

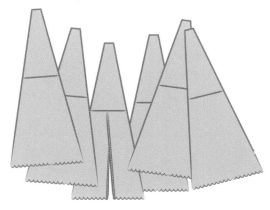

4 Pin the lower edge of another top piece to the upper edge of a bottom piece, with right sides together and raw edges even. Stitch a ³⁄₈in (1cm) seam, press open, and bind the seam allowances together. Repeat for the remaining top and bottom pieces. You should now have six full-length panels, including the one with the doors.

5 Pin a panel to the door panel along the long edges, with right sides together, raw edges even, and the bound seam allowances matching. Pin one of the long ribbons into the pinned seam, 22in (56cm) up from the lower edge, with half the ribbon protruding on the inside and half on the outside. Stitch a ³⁄₈in (1cm) seam. Repeat to join a panel to the other long edge of the door panel, inserting the other long ribbon into this seam.

TIP FABRIC WITHOUT SCALLOPS
If your fabric doesn't have a scalloped edge, you can still make the wigwam in the same way, because the lower edge will be a selvage instead and so will not need finishing.

6 Join the other long edge of one of these two panels to the long edge of another panel in the same way as in step 5, but omitting the ribbon. Repeat this all the way around, until all six panels are joined along the long edges. Press the seams open.

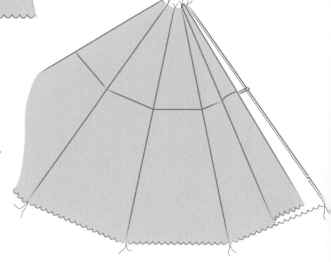

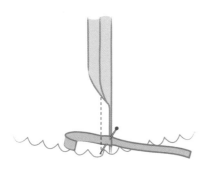

7 Fold one of the shorter ribbons in half crosswise and place the folded end at the bottom of one of the side seams, at right angles to it, encasing both seam allowances. Pin in place. Now pin three more ties over the seam in the same way, one 21in (54cm) away from the hem, one where the top piece of the panel meets the lower piece, and one 4in (10cm) from the top of the wigwam.

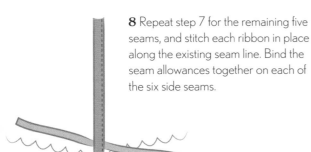

8 Repeat step 7 for the remaining five seams, and stitch each ribbon in place along the existing seam line. Bind the seam allowances together on each of the six side seams.

9 Now bind the top raw edge of the wigwam. Place a pole in the vise and drill a ¼in (5mm) hole 8in (20cm) from one end. Repeat for the other five poles. Thread strong string or jute through the holes and tie the poles together. Slot the tied-together ends of the poles through the opening at the top of the wigwam, splay the poles out, and pull the sides of the wigwam over the poles. On the inside, tie the ribbons around the poles to secure the fabric to the poles. Use the long ribbons at the front to tie the doors open.

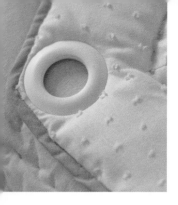

patchwork wigwam mat

This versatile hexagonal mat is designed to fit inside the six-sided Wigwam (see page 122). It has six grommets (eyelets) for the poles to fit through, but they could be omitted if you want to use it instead as a child's play mat or a picnic blanket. I used a delicate voile in subtle colors, but the design would also work well with vivid colors and contrasts.

you will need

Cotton voile or other fabric in up to five colors or patterns

Matching sewing thread

1¾yd (1.7m) cotton batting (wadding)

1¾yd (1.7m) each of fabric for front lining (if using voile for patchwork—see Tip), batting, and fabric for back lining

5½yd (5m) of bias tape (bias binding)

Six white plastic 1¼in (28mm) grommets (eyelets)

Contrasting embroidery floss (thread)

dimensions

The finished mat is 62½in (160cm) across.

1 Using the five templates on page 143 that together form one of the six large triangles making up the hexagon, and adding a ³⁄₈in (1cm) seam all around, cut out six fabric pieces from each template. Either use a different color of fabric for each template, or alternate the colors, or use just one color for all the templates—whichever you prefer.

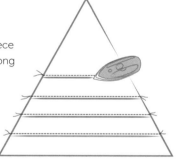

2 Divide the fabric pieces into six sets, with one piece from each template per set. For each set, join the long edges of the pieces in descending size, pinning them with right sides together and stitching ³⁄₈in (1cm) seams. Each of the resulting six large triangles should have sides that all measure 32in (82cm). Press the seams open, then press them downward.

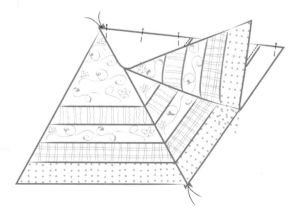

3 With right sides together, raw edges even, and seams matching, pin two triangles together. Stitch a ³⁄₈in (1cm) seam. Repeat for the remaining triangles until you have a complete hexagon. Press the seams open.

TIP OPAQUE FABRIC If you are using opaque fabric rather than voile for the patchwork, the front lining can be omitted, but you will still need the back lining.

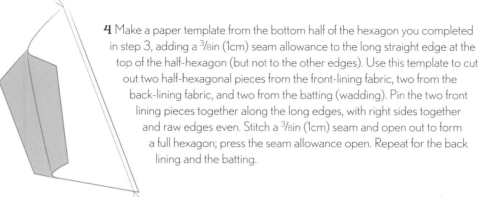

4 Make a paper template from the bottom half of the hexagon you completed in step 3, adding a ³⁄₈in (1cm) seam allowance to the long straight edge at the top of the half-hexagon (but not to the other edges). Use this template to cut out two half-hexagonal pieces from the front-lining fabric, two from the back-lining fabric, and two from the batting (wadding). Pin the two front lining pieces together along the long edges, with right sides together and raw edges even. Stitch a ³⁄₈in (1cm) seam and open out to form a full hexagon; press the seam allowance open. Repeat for the back lining and the batting.

5 Place the front lining right side up on top of the batting, and place the patchwork piece on top of this, again right side up. Trim the outer raw edges of the patchwork piece so they are even with the lining layers. Pin and then machine baste the three layers together all around the hexagon, ¼in (5mm) from the edge, pivoting the fabric at each corner. Place this padded and lined front on top of the back lining, wrong sides together. Pin around the edges and then machine baste again in the same way.

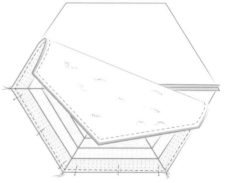

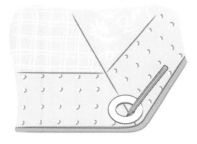

6 Bind all around the edges of the mat, as shown on page 12. Mark the positions of the grommets (eyelets) at each corner. Following the manufacturer's instructions, cut out the holes and insert the grommets. Hand baste the layers together and then hand quilt the mat using running stitch (see page 10) and embroidery floss (thread), ¼in (5mm) outside some of the seams stitched in step 2. Remove the basting.

garden kneeler

Take the weight off your knees with this fully padded pretty garden kneeler or sit on it for a welcome garden break. Made out of wipe-clean oilcloth and with two sturdy handles, it is a lovely practical addition to your garden tools. When not in use, it also adds a lovely pop of print and color to your garden shed!

you will need

Two 12in (31cm) lengths of 1in- (25mm-) wide twill tape

One 16 x 21in (40 x 54cm) rectangle each of two oilcloth fabrics

Matching sewing thread

9oz (250g) of 100 percent polyester high-loft fiberfill toy filling

1 Pin one length of twill tape to the right side of one oilcloth rectangle, as shown, so that the ends of the tape are even with one short edge of the oilcloth and are equal distances from the long edges. Make sure that the pins are no more than $3/8$ in (1cm) from the edge. Repeat to pin the other length of tape to the other short edge of the same piece. Stitch each handle in place $3/8$in (1cm) from the edge.

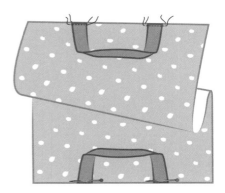

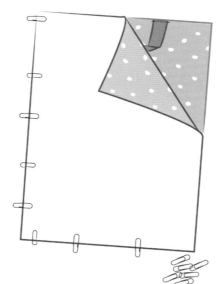

2 Place the other oilcloth rectangle on top of the first one, with right sides together, sandwiching the handles between the two layers. Paperclip in place around the edges, rather than pinning.

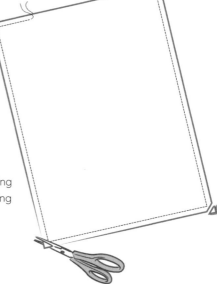

3 Using a Teflon foot on your machine (see Tips), and starting and finishing at one of the shorter sides, stitch a $3/8$in (1cm) seam, pivoting the fabric at the corners and leaving an opening between the starting and finishing points. Snip off the corners of the seam allowances.

SEWING ON OILCLOTH

The hardest part of sewing oilcloth is that the foot grips the oilcloth and can stop you from sewing evenly. A Teflon foot on the sewing machine offsets this. Keeping your stitches large also helps.

Avoid using pins on areas that will be visible, as they leave lasting holes—use paperclips instead.

4 Turn the kneeler right side out through the opening. Using a blunt-ended tool, such as the rounded end of a chopstick, carefully push out the corners. Take a generous handful of filling and gently pull it to loosen it, repeating the process two or three times. Insert it into the cover, starting in one of the corners farthest from the opening. Gently, but firmly, push the filling into the corner. Repeat with the other corner farthest from the opening, then fill the remaining two corners. Insert small amounts of additional filling, gradually working toward the opening, until it is firm and plump. Fold in the seam allowances of the opening, and paperclip the opening closed, then stitch it using a Teflon foot.

gardener's apron

Every gardener needs an apron, to keep everything at hand and to protect clothing. Made from hardwearing canvas and oilcloth, this gardener's apron includes three deep storage pockets that will easily hold seed packets, plant labels, garden gloves, and hand tools.

you will need

One 23¼ x 7in (59 x 18cm) rectangle of oilcloth A for pocket panel

1¾yd (1.6m) of ½in- (15mm-) wide bias tape (bias binding)

One 15¼ x 11¼in (39 x 28.5cm) rectangle of oilcloth B for front panel

One 15¼ x 2¼in (39 x 6cm) strip of oilcloth A for front strip

One 15¼ x 12½in (39 x 32cm) rectangle of canvas for back

Matching sewing thread

Two silver ¾in (18mm) grommets (eyelets)

2¼yd (2m) of 1in- (2.5cm-) wide cotton tape

1 Using the templates on pages 140–141, fold the fabric pieces in half, and cut out one pocket panel and one front from the oilcloth rectangles and one back from the canvas rectangle, all on the fold. There is no need to add seam allowances. Instead of pins, use paperclips on the oilcloth (see Tips on page 129). Use the bias tape (bias binding) to bind the top edge of the pocket, as shown on page 12. With a water-soluble pen, mark on the right side of the pocket panel the fold lines and placement lines shown on the template.

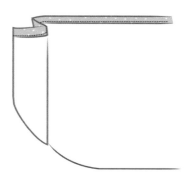

2 Near each side edge of the pocket panel, make a knife pleat using the three lines near the edge as a guide. To do this, make an outer fold (with wrong sides together) along the outer fold line, then make an inner fold (with right sides together) along the inner fold line, and finally bring the outer fold over to the placement line. Use paperclips to hold the pleats in place. Lightly press the folds from the wrong side of the oilcloth.

3 Each of the two inverted pleats flanking the central pocket consists of two knife pleats that meet in the middle at a mutual placement line, so follow the same folding procedure as in step 2.

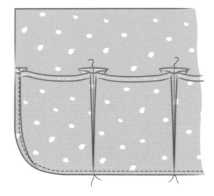

4 Place the pleated pocket panel, right side up, on the right side of the oilcloth front, matching the side and lower edges. Stitch the pocket panel in place from top to bottom, along the placement line that runs down the middle of each of the two inverted pleats you made in step 3. With the pleats in position, paperclip and then machine baste the pocket panel to the front, ¼in (5mm) from the side/lower edge.

5 With right sides together and raw edges even, paperclip one long edge of the front strip to the upper edge of the front panel. Stitch a ³⁄₈in (1cm) seam. Open out the front so that the strip is above the front panel, and finger press the seam open.

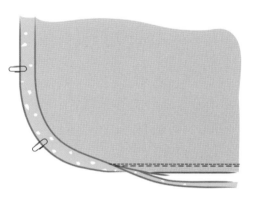

6 With right sides together and raw edges even, paperclip the front to the back along the top edge. Stitch a ³⁄₈in seam along this edge. Finger press the seam open. Turn right side out.

7 With wrong sides together and raw edges even, paperclip the front to the back around the side/lower edge. Starting at the top left corner, bind the raw edges as shown on page 12 – take your time doing this, stretching the bias tape (bias binding) around the curves as you go.

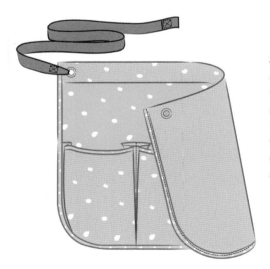

8 Mark the position of the grommets (eyelets) at each top corner and, following the manufacturer's instructions, insert the grommets. Cut the length of tape in half. At one end, turn under 1in (2.5cm) and then the same amount again, so that the raw edge is tucked inside. Stitch in place, using an "X" within a rectangle as shown, then repeat for the other length of tape. Thread the unfinished end of one tape through a grommet, then turn under 1in (2.5cm) twice and pin this to the portion of the tape on the other side of the grommet. Stitch in place as before. Repeat for the other length of tape and the second grommet.

doily bunting

I love bunting and have made quite a variety over the years, but my favorite by far is this pretty bunting made from up-cycled crochet doilies and butterflies found at garage sales and flea markets. Super quick and easy to make, the bunting can be dyed to match your color theme.

1 Following the manufacturer's instructions, dye the crochet doilies and butterflies using the cold-water dye. Leave to dry, then fold each dyed doily in half and cut along the fold.

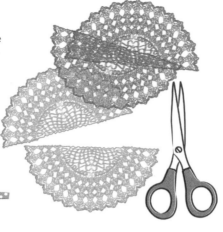

you will need

Cotton crochet doilies of different sizes

Cotton crochet butterflies

Cold-water dye

½in- (15mm-) wide bias tape (bias binding)

2 If the bias tape (bias binding) doesn't already have a central fold, fold it in half lengthwise, wrong sides together, and press the fold. Starting and finishing about 6in (15cm) from the ends of the tape, pin the doilies and butterflies in place, leaving gaps between them.

3 Stitch the two halves of the bias tape together near the bottom edge, catching in the doilies and the butterflies' wings.

4 Fold over each end of the bias tape to create a large loop, and stitch in place.

templates

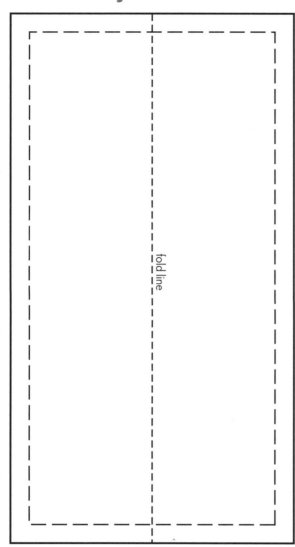

fold line

cook's apron (p32)

MAIN PIECE
Enlarge to four times this size.
Cut 1 from canvas.
³⁄₈in (1cm) seam/hem
allowances included.

◎ grommet (eyelet) position

outer fold line

place on fold

pocket position

BAND
Enlarge to twice this size.
Cut 1 each from canvas and interfacing.
³⁄₈in (1cm) seam allowance included.

linen basket (p88)

BASE
Enlarge to twice this size.
Cut 1 each from linen, lining, and stiff interfacing,
and cut 2 from heavyweight interfacing.
$^3/_8$in (1cm) seam allowance included.

lavender tags
(p76)

Full size.
Cut 2 from fabric for each tag—
omit seam allowance if using felt.
$^1/_4$in (5mm) seam allowance
included (not needed for felt).

double oven mitt (p36)

place on fold

MITT
Enlarge to twice this size.
Cut 2 each from canvas, lining,
and batting (wadding).

BACK OF MITT
Enlarge to twice this size.
Cut 2 from canvas and
1 from batting (wadding).

eye mask
(p108)
Enlarge to twice this size.
Cut 1 each from fabric, lining,
and batting (wadding).

potholder (p39)

ROUNDED CORNER
Full size.
Use to round 4 corners of each square
and 2 corners of each rectangle.

patchwork ottoman pouf (p56)

SIDE PIECE
Enlarge to twice this size.
Cut 16 from fabric.
⅜in (1cm) seam allowance
included.

TOP CENTER CIRCLE
Enlarge to twice this size.
Cut 1 each from fabric and interfacing.

WEDGE
Enlarge to twice this size.
Cut 16 from fabric.
⅜in (1cm) seam
allowance included.

LARGE ROSE
Full size.
Cut 5 from felt.

rose
brooch (p28)

SMALL ROSE
Full size.
Cut 2 from felt.

clothespin basket (p91)

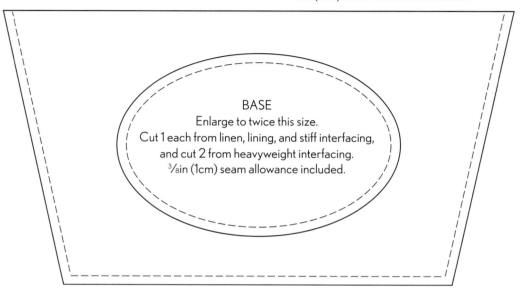

SIDE PIECE
Enlarge to twice this size.
Cut 2 each from linen and lining, and
cut 4 from heavyweight interfacing.
³⁄₈in (1cm) seam allowance included.

BASE
Enlarge to twice this size.
Cut 1 each from linen, lining, and stiff interfacing,
and cut 2 from heavyweight interfacing.
³⁄₈in (1cm) seam allowance included.

gardener's apron (p130)

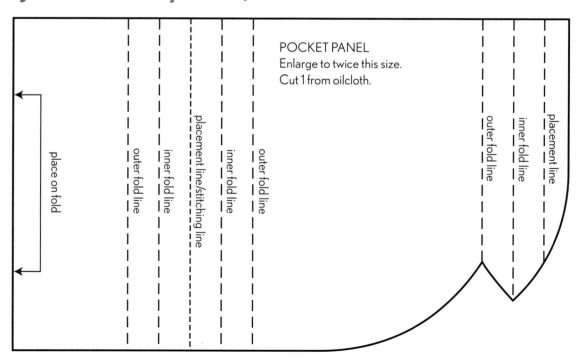

POCKET PANEL
Enlarge to twice this size.
Cut 1 from oilcloth.

place on fold

outer fold line

inner fold line

placement line/stitching line

inner fold line

outer fold line

outer fold line

inner fold line

placement line

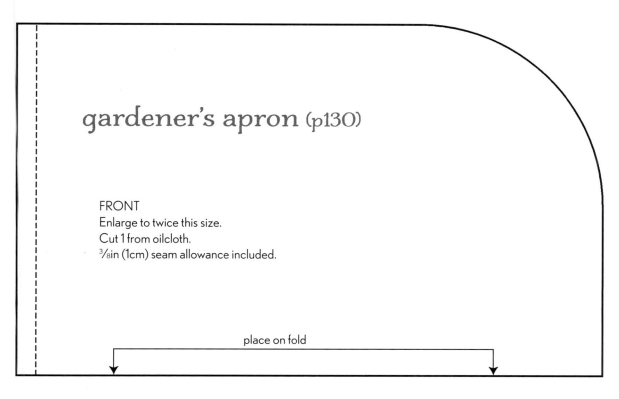

gardener's apron (p130)

FRONT
Enlarge to twice this size.
Cut 1 from oilcloth.
$^{3}/_{8}$in (1cm) seam allowance included.

place on fold

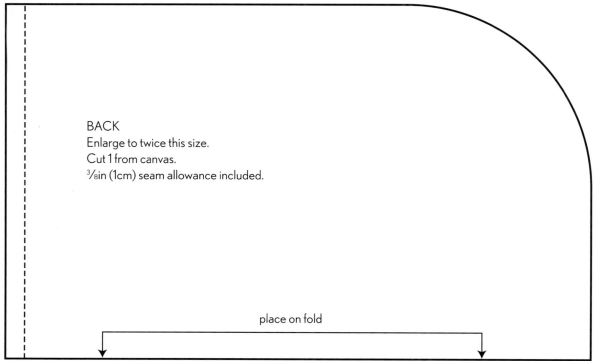

BACK
Enlarge to twice this size.
Cut 1 from canvas.
$^{3}/_{8}$in (1cm) seam allowance included.

place on fold

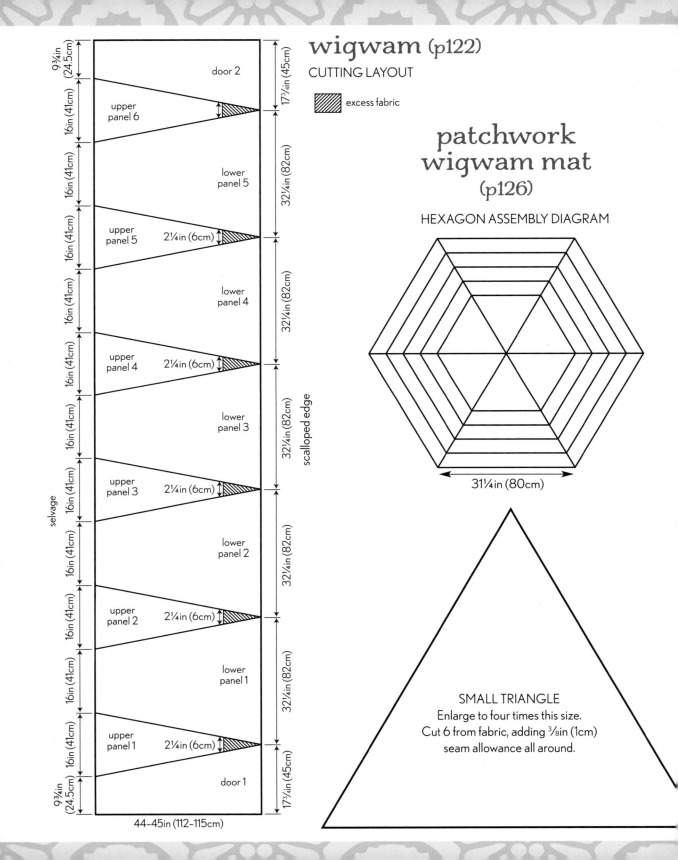

wigwam (p122)

CUTTING LAYOUT

▨ excess fabric

patchwork wigwam mat (p126)

HEXAGON ASSEMBLY DIAGRAM

door 2

upper panel 6

lower panel 5

upper panel 5   2¼in (6cm)

lower panel 4

upper panel 4   2¼in (6cm)

lower panel 3

upper panel 3   2¼in (6cm)

lower panel 2

upper panel 2   2¼in (6cm)

lower panel 1

upper panel 1   2¼in (6cm)

door 1

9¾in (24.5cm)

16in (41cm)

16in (41cm)

16in (41cm)

16in (41cm)

16in (41cm)

16in (41cm)

16in (41cm)

16in (41cm)

16in (41cm)

16in (41cm)

16in (41cm)

16in (41cm)

9¾in (24.5cm)

selvage

17¾in (45cm)

32¼in (82cm)

32¼in (82cm)

32¼in (82cm)

scalloped edge

32¼in (82cm)

32¼in (82cm)

32¼in (82cm)

17¾in (45cm)

44–45in (112–115cm)

31¼in (80cm)

SMALL TRIANGLE
Enlarge to four times this size.
Cut 6 from fabric, adding ⅜in (1cm)
seam allowance all around.

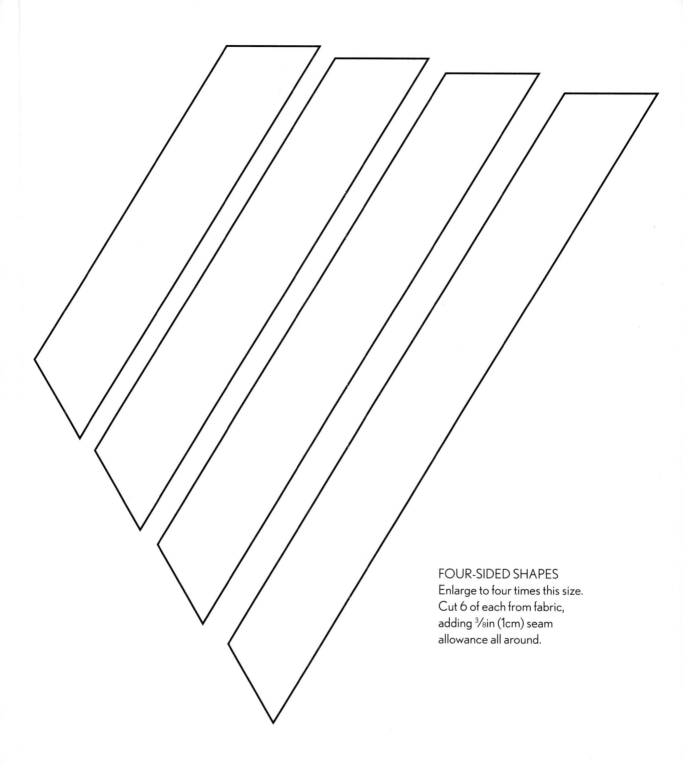

FOUR-SIDED SHAPES
Enlarge to four times this size.
Cut 6 of each from fabric,
adding ³⁄₈in (1cm) seam
allowance all around.

resources

Torie Jayne's website
www.toriejayne.com

Cotton canvas printed fabrics
available from Torie Jayne's
Spoonflower Store (which ships
worldwide)
www.spoonflower.com/profiles/torie
_jayne

Linen from Ada & Ina
www.linenfabrics.co.uk

Vintage fabrics and trims from
The Linen Garden
www.thelinengarden.co.uk

Bridal leather used for handles
from eBay seller Leatherworld
www.ebay.co.uk/usr/leatherworld

Wool felt squares in pale green,
raspberry, and natural from eBay
seller Tilly0412
www.ebay.co.uk/usr/tilly0412

Crochet lace trim and pompom
trim from Sass & Belle
www.sassandbelle.co.uk

Pine dowels used in wigwam from
eBay seller lovethresholds
www.ebay.co.uk/usr/lovethresholds

Narrow rickrack, lilac polka-dot
binding, mini pompom trim from
Elephant in my Handbag
www.elephantinmyhandbag.com

Oilcloth in gray with white polka-
dots and in aqua with white
polka-dots from Clarke & Clarke
www.clarke-clarke.co.uk

Vinyl- (PVC-) coated fabric in duck
egg blue with white polka-dots
from Laura Ashley
www.lauraashley.com/uk

Grosgrain ribbon from
Jane Means
www.janemeans.com

Herringbone tape, cotton in duck
egg blue, felt in peach, dobby
stripe, and dotted swiss from
Sooz Custom Clothing
www.soozcustomclothing.co.uk

Budgie embroidered appliqué
from Petra Boase
www.petraboase.com

Crochet flowers from
Rockin' Beads
www.rockinbeads.co.uk

Quilting supplies from
Cowslip Workshops
www.cowslipworkshops.co.uk

CRAFT STOCKISTS:
UK & Europe

Panduro Hobby
www.pandurohobby.co.uk

Hobbycraft
www.hobbycraft.co.uk

John Lewis
www.johnlewis.com

CRAFT STOCKISTS: USA

Michaels
www.michaels.com

Jo-Ann
www.joann.com

Rough Linen
www.roughlinen.com

index